FIRST AID FOR THE

MATCH

INSIDER *FROM STUDENTS AND RESIDENCY DIRECTORS* ADVICE

First Edition

TAO LE, MD

University of California, San Francisco, Class of 1996
Yale-New Haven Hospital, Resident in Internal Medicine

VIKAS BHUSHAN, MD

University of California, San Francisco, Class of 1991
Diagnostic Radiologist

CHIRAG AMIN, MD

University of Miami, Class of 1996
Orlando Regional Medical Center
Resident in Orthopaedic Surgery

CONTRIBUTORS

KIEU NGUYEN, MD

University of California, San Francisco, Class of 1995
Loma Linda University, Resident in Emergency Medicine

DAVID ALTMAN, MD

Associate Dean of Medical Students, 1982-1989
University of California, San Francisco

APPLETON & LANGE

STAMFORD, CONNECTICUT

Copyright 1997 by Appleton & Lange

99 00 / 10 9 8 7 6 5 4 3

Prentice Hall International (UK) Limited, *London*
Prentice Hall of Australia Pty. Limited, *Sydney*
Prentice Hall Canada, Inc., *Toronto*
Prentice Hall Hispanoamericana, S.A., *Mexico*
Prentice Hall of India Private Limited, *New Delhi*
Prentice Hall of Japan, Inc., *Tokyo*
Simon & Schuster Asia Pte. Ltd., *Singapore*
Editora Prentice Hall do Brasil Ltda., *Rio de Janeiro*
Prentice Hall, *Englewood Cliffs, New Jersey*

Acquisitions Editor: Marinita S. Timban
Production Services: Rainbow Graphics, Inc.
Designer: Design Group Cook

PRINTED IN THE UNITED STATES OF AMERICA

ISBN 0-8385-2596-2

To the contributors to this and future editions, who took
time to share their experience, advice, and
humor for the benefit of students.

&

To our families, friends, and loved ones, who endured
and assisted in the task of assembling this guide.

Table of Contents

Foreword

There are predictable times in the course of medical education that will engender in nearly every student some combination of excitement, anxiety, and dread. The *First Aid* series aims to assist students through these times by providing sound, thoughtful, student-oriented guidance and advice, and *First Aid for the Match* continues this tradition. *First Aid for the USMLE Step 1* has fulfilled these goals and has reached an audience of more than 80,000 medical students in five years.

As Dean of Students at a distinguished school of medicine for a number of years, I had the pleasure of working with over a thousand medical students in their passage through the exercises of career choice, residency selection, and negotiation of the challenges of the "Match." I was responsible for writing all of their deans' letters—letters seen by both the subjects and the recipients as having both critical importance and dubious value. Each student brought to the process their hopes and fears, their pride and their (sometimes not very hidden) insecurities. There is no doubt that the choice of specialty and the choice of residency program are of major consequence. Yet faculty advisers and student affairs deans are rarely entirely up to the task of providing students facing these choices with the information and advice called for. And not surprisingly, students often wonder whether the advice being given is to some degree driven by the faculty's own concerns and wishes rather than entirely in the students' interests.

First Aid for the Match provides its readers with much of the key facts and advice needed to work through this process. It cannot and should not substitute for the valuable advice and counsel that students can best receive from faculty advisers and members of the dean's staff. And it cannot replace the currency of "word of mouth" information received from student colleagues and residents who have recently survived these challenges. However, it successfully supplements these sources with recent, verified data about residency selection, up-to-date information about the various core residency training specialties, helpful tips on selecting both specialties and residencies, and useful guidance concerning such critical events as writing a personal statement, being interviewed, and succeeding in the match process itself.

The essence of this process is that every party involved is hoping for the best possible results. The residency program certainly wants to acquire an outstanding new crop of house staff, to maintain the program's pride, to provide assurance that faculty will be well challenged by the best and brightest, and to ensure that patients will receive the best possible medical care. The medical school wants to ensure that its graduates achieve their highest choices, both for its own pride and traditions and so that incoming students can be assured that they will be well taken care of at the other end of their medical school experience. Lastly, and for whom this book is written, are the students going through the match process who see this as a critical step that can determine their future professional happiness and success.

How many of these goals are actually achieved certainly varies from program to program, school to school, and student to student. How many of those hoped-for results are actually determined by the Match is also not clear. What is certain is that students armed with current information resources such as *First Aid for the Match* generally do better in the residency application process.

The authors are anxious for your feedback and are committed to maintaining the currency of this book through these times of rapid change. I wish all the readers of this guide and all those going through the process of the Match the very best of luck and professional and personal success.

David F. Altman, M.D.
Associate Dean of Medical Students, 1982–1989
University of California San Francisco

Preface

Going through the residency application process can be a confusing, time-consuming, even hazardous adventure. If you make the right decisions, you will most likely find a residency position that suits you best. A bad or uninformed decision can derail your career and waste years of your life. The purpose of *First Aid for the Match* is to help medical students effectively and efficiently navigate the residency application process. This book helps students make the most of their limited time, money, and energy. In the spirit of *First Aid for the USMLE Step 1*, this book is a student-to-student guide that draws on the advice and experiences of medical students who have successfully gone through the Match and are now training in the programs of their choice. *First Aid for the Match* has a number of unique features that make it indispensable to the residency applicant:

- Insider advice from medical students and residency program directors.
- The latest trends in the residency application process and specialty fields.
- Application and interview tips tailored to each specialty.
- Real personal statements and résumés that worked.
- A student-tested guide to cheap, efficient interview travel and lodging.
- Common interview questions with suggested strategies for responding to each.
- Emergency protocols for the Scramble (if you do not match).
- A master checklist for the application process.

First Aid for the Match is meant to be a guide rather than a comprehensive source of information. It should supplement information and advice provided by other students, your adviser, and your dean's office. Though the material has been reviewed by medical faculty and students, errors and omissions are inevitable. We urge readers to suggest improvements and identify inaccuracies. We invite students and faculty to continue sharing their thoughts and ideas to help us improve *First Aid for the Match* (see How to Contribute, p. xv).

New Haven   Tao Le
Los Angeles   Vikas Bhushan
Orlando   Chirag Amin
July, 1996

Acknowledgments

We owe special thanks to Dr. Lawrence Tierney, Dr. Stephen McPhee, Dr. Helen Loesser, Dr. Anthony Glaser, Dr. Eric Schulze, Thao Pham, Dr. Daniel Lowenstein, Dr. Denise Rodgers, Dr. Linda Ferrell, Henry Nguyen, Dr. Richard Odom, Dr. Patricia Robertson, Uzma Samadani, David Steensma, Dr. Lisa Alsta, Dr. Daniela Drake, Dr. Sana Khan, and the UCSF School of Medicine Office of Student Affairs for their thoughtful comments, corrections, and advice.

Thanks to our editor Marinita Timban for her enthusiasm, support, and commitment to the First Aid books. Thanks to Jeanne Gahagan and Johnie Kelly for their tireless administrative assistance. For support and encouragement throughout the process, we are grateful to Ray Moloney (PaperBook Press) and Jonathan Kirsch.

For submitting feedback and contributions, we thank David Anick, Satish Batchu, Perry Brown, Carrie Chen, Eddie Frothingham, Anna Hejinian, Tony Hill, Catherine Hoffman, Clara Hsu, Bruce Lattyak, Mark Lee, Rick Miller, Sonia Nagy, Elizabeth Oudens, Noel Saks, Dennis Shay, Jacque Slaughter, Lisa Strate, Mel Stone, Dax Swanson, Judy Tjoe, and Margo Vener.

How to Contribute

First Aid for the Match incorporates many contributions and changes from students and faculty. We invite you to participate in this process.

Please send us:

* Strategies for applying and interviewing in your specialty.
* Your personal statement and CV (feel free to edit or mask for privacy).
* Anecdotes of your application and interviewing experiences.
* Your medical school's guide to the Match.
* Corrections and clarifications.

Personalized contributions (i.e., anecdotes and personal statements), if used, will be altered to protect the identity of the contributor. For each entry incorporated into the next edition, you will receive a $10 coupon per entry good toward the purchase of any Appleton & Lange medical book, as well as personal acknowledgment in the next edition. Significant contributions will be compensated at the discretion of the publisher.

The preferred way to submit suggestions and corrections is via electronic mail, addressed to:

Firstaid99@aol.com

Correspondence with the authors can be addressed to Tao Le (taodoc@aol.com), Vikas Bhushan (vbhushan@aol.com) or Chirag Amin (chiragamin@aol.com). You can also use the contribution and survey forms on the following pages. Attach additional pages as needed. Please send your contributions and corrections, neatly written or typed to: First Aid for the Match, Appleton & Lange, Four Stamford Plaza, P.O. Box 120041, Stamford, CT 06912-0041.

Note to Contributors

All entries are subject to editing and reviewing. Please verify all data and spellings carefully. In the event that similar or duplicate entries are received, only the first entry received will be used. Please follow the style, punctuation, and format of this edition if possible.

Contribution Form

For tips and strategies for
applying and interviewing
in your specialty.

Contributor Name: _____

School/Affiliation: _____

Address: _____

_____

Telephone: _____

Your specialty: _____

Type of program where you matched: __ Clinical
                                       __ Academic

Region where you applied (e.g., Northeast, both coasts): _____

Application trends in your specialty:

Application tips for your specialty:

Interview tips for your specialty:

Specialty resources (e.g., useful books, articles, directories on the specialty):

Other comments:

Please return by April 15th following the Match. You will receive personal acknowledgment and a $10 coupon toward selected Appleton & Lange books for material used in future editions.

User Survey

Contributor Name: _____

School/Affiliation: _____

Address: _____

_____

Telephone: _____

What student-to-student advice would you give someone going through the application process?

What would you change about the specialty overviews, application tips, interviewing tips, and specialty resources in Chapter 3?

What would you change about the application, personal statement, and CV tips?

What travel and interviewing tips would you change or add?

Is there an interesting application or interviewing experience that you would like to share?

How else would you improve *First Aid for the Match*? Any comments or suggestions? What did you like most about the book?

Please return by April 15th following the Match. You will receive personal acknowledgment and a $10 coupon toward selected Appleton & Lange books for material used in future editions.

The Match

INTRODUCTION

Relax.

This chapter will help to familiarize you with the Match. Our goal is to minimize your stress, maximize the fruits of your efforts, and improve your chances of landing an optimal residency position. As a medical student, you undoubtedly remember the process of medical school applications and interviews. However, the Match has different rules and strategies. The entire process can be overwhelming; each year, some students end up in an unsatisfactory program or unmatched, wondering what went wrong on Match Day. It is easy to lose sight of your goals and not obtain the residency position you desire. And since most students go through the Match only once, mistakes can lead to a lifetime of regret.

The Match is a giant "computer dating game" of sorts. But the fact that this relationship is an intimate one that lasts for 3 years or more means you need to ensure that your potential partner has compatible goals and interests. Conversely, directors of residency programs are searching for the best students. Therefore, you must know the right moves and when to make them. Asking how much the pay is for a resident is akin to asking a date his or her weight. You may be dying to know, but discretion is key.

Of course, the two biggest fears are (1) not matching at any program; and (2) ending up in a program that makes you miserable. Approximately 8% of the U.S. and Canadian participants and 60% of the non-U.S. foreign graduates in the National Residency Matching Program (NRMP) were "stood up" on the big day in 1996. Conversely, over 16% of the available NRMP positions in "less competitive" residencies remained unfilled. Common mistakes that students make when going through the Match process include the following:

- ▶ Not understanding the details of the Match for a particular specialty
- ▶ Starting the application process too late
- ▶ Applying to or ranking too few programs to ensure a match
- ▶ Letting the application paperwork overwhelm you
- ▶ Ignoring key NRMP publications

> ASKING HOW MUCH THE PAY IS FOR A RESIDENT IS AKIN TO ASKING A DATE HIS OR HER WEIGHT.

- ▶ Submitting a weak personal statement and curriculum vitae
- ▶ Not knowing what to look for in a residency training program
- ▶ Preparing inadequately for residency interviews
- ▶ Ranking programs on the basis of probability of acceptance rather than desirability
- ▶ Panicking after failing to match, rather than intelligently playing the "Scramble"

In this chapter, we will help you understand the Match to guard you against these common pitfalls.

WHAT IS THE MATCH?

Although there are actually several matches, most people know the NRMP as **the** Match. The NRMP offers positions in a wide range of specialties (Table 1–1), including some specialties with their own matches. With over 90% of all graduating U.S. and Canadian medical students participating, as well as a surprisingly high number of international medical graduates, the NRMP is the largest match by far (Figure 1–1).

The basic modus operandi of the Match is as follows. After the interview season, residency training programs submit a list of applicants in the order in which they would offer acceptances; students enter lists of programs in the order in which they would accept offers. Both students and programs submit their rankings to the NRMP. Then, in a matter of minutes, a computer program matches the student to the highest program on his or her list that offered a position. The Match usually occurs in late February; the results

| | TABLE 1–1. Specialties with their own matches. | |
Specialty	Matching Program	Month of Match Day
Dermatology	National Residency Matching Program 2450 N Street NW, Suite 201 Washington, DC 20037-1141 202-828-0566	October after graduation
Neurology	Neurology Matching Program P.O. Box 7999 San Francisco, CA 94120 415-923-3907	January of senior year
Neurosurgery	Neurosurgical Surgery Matching Program P.O. Box 7999 San Francisco, CA 94120 415-923-3907	January of senior year
Ophthalmology	Ophthalmology Matching Program P.O. Box 7999 San Francisco, CA 94120 415-923-3907	January of senior year
Otolaryngology	Otolaryngology Matching Program P.O. Box 7999 San Francisco, CA 94120 415-923-3907	January of senior year
Urology	AUA Residency Matching Program 6900 Fannin, Suite 546 Houston, TX 77030 713-665-7500	Late January of senior year

FIGURE 1-1

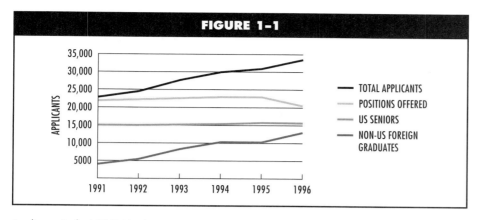

Applicants in the NRMP Match.

are then announced simultaneously across the country on "Match Day" in mid-March. In 1996, 33,500 applicants enrolled in the Match, of the 24,718 applicants who submitted rank lists, 18,007 received offers (Figure 1–2).

If you are a U.S. medical student, you automatically receive information about the NRMP Match through your school in the spring of your third year. However, the NRMP can be contacted directly for more information at:

National Residency Matching Program
2450 N Street NW, Suite 201
Washington, DC 20037-1141
(202) 828-0676 for U.S. seniors
(202) 828-0566 for independent applicants

WHY IS THERE A MATCH?

By the late 1940s, the traditional matching process was growing increasingly chaotic. There were almost twice as many residency positions as there were U.S. medical graduates. More competitive programs had the luxury of receiving and reviewing large batches of applications before doling out their residency spots late in the students' fourth year. Less competitive programs tried to get a head start by asking students to commit to the program early in the fourth year or even during the third year.

As a result, students were forced to gamble by deciding whether to accept an early offer from a less competitive program and forfeit a later shot at better programs or to pass up the early offer and risk not being accepted in a better program. Residency directors faced a similar dilemma. If they filled all their positions too early, they would not be able to offer a position to a more desirable candidate who applied later; however, if they held out for better applicants, they risked not filling their programs.

As a solution to these dilemmas, the first Match was held in 1952. It was a huge success, with over 98% of the residency programs and 97% of the students participating. The Match eliminated guessing games for the most part by allowing applicants and programs to rank each other on the basis of desirability. The algorithm used to match applicants with programs has remained largely unchanged over the years. For a simple explanation of how the matching algorithm works, see Chapter 10.

FIGURE 1-2

33,500
enrolled

↓

25,000
rank lists

↓

20,500
PGY-1 positions
available

↓

18,000
matched

Flowchart of the NRMP Match.

WHAT OTHER MATCHES ARE THERE?

Though the NRMP is the largest matching program available to American medical students and international medical graduates, there are other matches as well, including some that operate independently of the NRMP.

Specialties With Their Own Matches

Some specialties have their own match processes with different match days. These specialties include dermatology, neurology, ophthalmology, otolaryngology, and urology. Note that dermatology has a much later match (see Table 1–1). Except for dermatology and urology, these specialty matches are run by Dr. August Colenbrander, an ophthalmologist in San Francisco. Since many of these specialties require training in medicine, pediatrics, or surgery, most applicants also match through the NRMP for 1 or 2 years of transitional training before starting their specialty work. Many students aiming for these specialties also apply for another specialty in the NRMP Match as a backup (eg, general surgery as a backup for neurosurgery). Please refer to "Your Specialty and the Match" (pg. 19) for more specific matching information regarding your target specialty.

NRMP Couples Match

In the couples match, the NRMP allows any two people to be matched with residency programs in the same geographic area if they so desire. Any two people can apply as a couple. Partners apply and interview separately at programs in the same geographic region. They then submit a rank-order list of pairs of programs in the order in which they would accept offers. Because couples are often limited by geography, they often submit more applications to maximize the likelihood of a successful match. To help matters more, the rank-order list gives a couple the option of seeking matches in separate locations or allowing one partner to go unmatched if a couples match is not possible.

Some residency directors and deans believe that many couples do better together in the Match than if they were to apply and match separately. Couples tend to be viewed as more stable and less likely to leave residency programs. Because of the hassles of moving again after residency, especially with kids, couples are more likely to contribute to the faculty pool of the institution where they trained. If a couple targets a program in the same specialty and one partner is more desirable, the residency selection will often move the less competitive partner higher on the rank-order list rather than dropping the more competitive partner (though the reverse can occur). In short, couples may have advantages in the Match, though it's probably no reason to start a relationship! Internship will be tough enough as is. For more information about the couples match, consult the section on "Special Cases" in your *NRMP Handbook for Students*.

Shared-Schedule Match

Shared-schedule positions in the NRMP Match allow two people to share the duties and responsibilities of one residency position. An applicant enrolls individually in the NRMP Match and then pairs up with a partner (eg, a significant other) by completing a *Shared Residency Pair Form*, due in the fall preceding Match Day. The pair shares one NRMP applicant code, applies and interviews together, and submits a single rank-order list. Though

ANY TWO PEOPLE CAN APPLY AS A COUPLE.

COUPLES MAY HAVE SOME ADVANTAGES OVER OTHER APPLICANTS IN THE MATCH.

each person spends less than full time working (eg, alternate months on rotation), both will spend more time in residency and will eventually do as much if not more work than a full-time resident. Many applicants seek shared-schedule positions because of family responsibilities or research, among other reasons. Consult "Special Cases" in your *NRMP Handbook for Students* for more information.

Canadian Match

The Canadian Residency Matching Service (CaRMS) was founded in 1970. Like its U.S. counterpart, the CaRMS Match is an orderly approach to matching applicants to their top choices and residency programs to their preferred applicants. In fact, CaRMS uses the same matching algorithm as the NRMP. CaRMS Match Day is also in mid-March. Approximately 1500 Canadian students apply for about 1500 slots annually offered through the Canadian Match. CaRMS is open to U.S. seniors, though few apply. For more information, contact:

Canadian Residency Matching Service
151 Slater Street, Suite 802
Ottawa, Ontario, Canada K1P 5H3
(800) 465-4584

Osteopathic Match

The Intern Registration Program, the osteopathic version of the Match, is run by the National Matching Services (NMS). All osteopathic graduates are required to take a 1-year osteopathic rotating internship approved by the American Osteopathic Association (AOA) before entering an osteopathic residency. Applicants interview in late summer and fall, submit a rank-order list by early January, and await results on the osteopathic Match Day in late January.

About 2200 osteopathic internships and 1100 residency positions are offered through the osteopathic match every year. Osteopathic residency directors have recently had more difficulty filling their positions, as osteopathic graduates have gained wider acceptance in allopathic residency programs and the AOA has relaxed its restrictions on osteopathic graduates pursuing allopathic training through the NRMP Match.

For more information, contact:

American Osteopathic Association
Department of Education
142 E. Ontario Street
Chicago, IL 60611
Phone (800) 621-1773, ext 7426

National Matching Service
Box 1208
Lewiston, NY 14092-8208
Phone (716) 282-4013
Fax (716) 282-0611

National Matching Service
595 Bay Street, Suite 300
Toronto, Ontario, Canada M5G 2C2
Phone (416) 977-3431
Fax (416) 977-5020

Armed Forces Match

Army, Navy, and Air Force residencies have their own matching process early in the senior year, several months earlier than the NRMP Match. Applicants usually have military service obligations (eg, graduates of Uniformed Services University of the Health Sciences School of Medicine and participants in the Health Professions Scholarship Program). After senior-year applicants have been interviewed, the military programs convene in late November and early December each year in a week-long affair known as "Selection Boards" to match programs and applicants. The nonmatch rate varies widely among the different services; nevertheless, simultaneous enrollment in the NRMP Match is highly recommended. All medical graduates of the Uniformed Services University are preferentially placed through an Armed Forces match. If you match with a military residency program, you are obliged to withdraw from the NRMP Match or from any other civilian match.

For more information on the Army military match, contact the regional AMEDD counselor.

For more information on the Air Force military match, contact:

Headquarters AFMPC/DPAME
550 C Street West, Suite 27
Randolph AFB, TX 78150-4729
(800) 531-5800
DSN 487-6331.

For more information on the Navy military match, contact:

Bureau of Medicine and Surgery
Code 512
Washington, DC 20372-5300
(202) 653-1318.

WHAT ARE MY CHANCES OF SUCCESS IN THE MATCH?

In general, U.S. seniors do well in the NRMP Match. About 80% of U.S. seniors obtain one of their first three choices each year (Table 1–2). The U.S. senior nonmatch rate has held steady at 6–7% for the past 10 years. In contrast, other applicants fare rather poorly (Table 1–3): In the 1995 Match, only one-half of the U.S. graduates (as opposed to U.S. seniors) and international medical graduates (IMGs) in the NRMP were successfully matched. IMGs, whether U.S. citizens or not, generally fare the worst. Foreign national IMGs in particular have experienced significant declines in match rates, from 63.4% in 1991 to 40.9% in 1995.

HOW DO I REGISTER FOR THE NRMP MATCH?

U.S. Seniors

In the spring of your third year of medical school, you will receive a preprinted student agreement form to review and sign. Make sure that the name listed on the agreement matches the name you use on your residency applications. The current registration fee is $25, payable to the NRMP, and is nonrefundable. Upon registering, you will be assigned an NRMP Applicant Code that you will use to identify yourself on residency applications

TABLE 1–2. Success of U.S. seniors in the 1995 NRMP Match.

Choice Obtained	Percent of Seniors
First	55.7
Second	14.5
Third	8.2
Fourth	5.1
> Fourth	9.7
Unmatched	6.8

TABLE 1–3. 1995 NRMP Match rate.

Applicant Type	PGY-1 Match Rate
U.S. seniors	92.1
Canadian students	69.0
U.S. graduates	51.3
Osteopaths	69.1
U.S. citizen foreign graduates	48.5
Non-U.S. foreign graduates	40.9

and correspondence. The deadline for registration is in July at the start of your senior year. Consult the current edition of the *NRMP Handbook for Students* for additional registration details.

U.S. Graduates

If you graduated from a U.S. medical school accredited through the Liaison Committee for Medical Education (LCME), you can register through your own school or another U.S. medical school. You can also enroll directly with the NRMP as an Independent Applicant (see below). If you are sponsored by a U.S. medical school, the school will serve as your NRMP "home base," from which to submit your rank-order list and where you will receive NRMP correspondence, including your Match results. Your *Agreement for Students or Sponsored Graduates* must be signed by both you and the dean of student affairs at your sponsor school. Your nonrefundable registration fee is also $25. Upon registering, you will receive an NRMP Applicant Code used to identify yourself on residency applications and in correspondence. The deadline for registering is in October before Match Day. See the current edition of the *NRMP Handbook for Students* for registration details.

Independent Applicants

The category of "independent applicants" includes several different groups: nonsponsored U.S. graduates, Canadian students/graduates, osteopathic students/graduates, and international medical graduates (IMGs). For information, contact the NRMP at (202) 828-0566 during the summer before the Match to receive the *NRMP Handbook for Independent Applicants*. To enroll, submit a completed *Independent Applicant Agreement* and $80, payable to the NRMP. The NRMP might also independently verify or request to see your credentials in order to approve your Match eligibility status. For example, IMGs need to pass the USMLE Step 1 and 2 as well as the English Test to participate in the Match.

Following registration, you will be assigned an NRMP Applicant Code, which you will use to identify yourself on residency applications and in correspondence. You will also receive a confidential Personal Identification Number (PIN). If you match at a program, your PIN will appear in the *USA Today* newspaper on Unmatch Day (the day before Match Day). The registration deadline is in October before Match Day. Consult the current edition of the *NRMP Handbook for Independent Applicants* for further details.

WHAT ABOUT THE OTHER MATCHES?

If you are a U.S. medical student, information pamphlets and registration materials for specialties outside the NRMP Match should be available at your dean's office. Otherwise, you can contact the specialty match programs directly for information and registration forms (Table 1–1). To register for the Armed Forces Match, contact your military branch's Medical Personnel Counselor or your local Armed Forces recruitment officer. Don't forget to register for the NRMP Match regardless of what other matches you enroll in. There is nothing to prevent you from enrolling in multiple matches; you just can't accept more than one appointment. Many of the non-NRMP matches require a preliminary transitional year obtained through the NRMP Match. In addition, many of these matches are very competitive, and the NRMP

ALWAYS ENROLL IN THE NRMP MATCH AS A BACKUP REGARDLESS OF WHAT OTHER MATCHES INTEREST YOU.

Match is a nice backup. It's better to register, match in advance, and lose the $25 fee than to be unable to participate in the Match at all.

NRMP PUBLICATIONS

The NRMP offers a slew of valuable publications that few students know about and fewer still take the time to read. A handbook and the *NRMP Directory* are distributed to every applicant upon registration. The rest can be ordered from the NRMP by calling (202)828-0416 or by filling out the NRMP Publications Order Form found in the back of the *NRMP Directory* and mailing it to:

ATTN: Membership and Publication Orders
National Residency Matching Program
2450 N Street, NW
Washington, DC 20037-1129

For each NRMP publication listed below, we include a list price, a description, and a rating based on utility.

NRMP Handbook for Students

This handbook is available free of charge through U.S. medical schools and is for U.S. seniors and sponsored graduates. Read it from cover to cover. It describes the NRMP and its role in the residency application process. You will be able to decipher the NRMP philosophy despite the stilted prose. The handbook has current details for registering for the Match and describes the couples match and shared-residency positions. It also supplies concise explanations for rank-order lists and supplemental rank lists. However, some of the juiciest information is stored in the appendices, including selected statistics from the previous Match, NRMP policy statements, and an explanation of the Match algorithm. Finally, the handbook's back cover lists key dates for the Match process.

NRMP Handbook for Independent Applicants

Like the *NRMP Handbook for Students*, this free publication from the NRMP is a must-read for independent applicants. You can get a copy by calling the NRMP at (202) 828-0566. The version for independent applicants covers the same topics as the general student handbook. In addition, the *Handbook for Independent Applicants* contains guidelines for verification of credentials for Match eligibility, a NRMP publication order form, and match dates for specialties covered in the NRMP's Specialties Matching Services (eg, dermatology).

NRMP Directory/Hospitals and Programs Participating in the Matching Program

The *NRMP Directory* is a catalog of residency programs participating in the Match. Part I of the directory organizes the programs by hospital. Use this section to see what other specialty training programs are offered at the hospitals you're interested in. For example, since the presence of an internal medicine program typically means a lower caliber of training for family practice residents, family practice applicants may want to find hospitals without medicine programs. Part II lists programs by specialty type and is much more useful. You should receive the edition for the previous Match at no cost upon registration. You will also receive a revised edition for your Match late in the fall.

NRMP Program Results/Listing of Filled and Unfilled Programs for the Match

If you want to find out which programs in your specialty were not filled last year, then this is the book to get. It's like going through someone's dirty laundry. The *NRMP Program Results* is given to unmatched applicants on Unmatch Day, who subsequently must enter the Scramble. Part II lists programs that did not fill all their spots. It can be a real eye-opener and give you a better feel for regional trends in competitiveness. If you are a marginal candidate applying in a competitive specialty, you may consider applying to several of the programs that went unfilled last year. But be forewarned—they probably went unfilled for good reasons. Though this publication is supposedly free only for applicants who failed to find placements in the previous Match, check your school's student affairs office for a copy.

NRMP Data

This must-have publication contains exhaustive data on the previous year's Match. It tracks Match trends over several years and puts you and your target specialty into perspective. Many of the tables are informative, but you'll want to check out a few choice ones (Table 1–4). Most students erroneously believe that the Match data are confidential. They aren't, if you can come up with $7 plus shipping, or if you choose to consult the copy in your school's student affairs office. Unfortunately, many student affairs offices operate on the belief that this data is confidential or that students don't really need these details.

Universal Application for Residency and Program Designation Card

You get one or two Universal Applications free when you sign up for the Match. There should be no need to purchase additional copies. Because you send a photocopy of the Universal Application to the few programs that accept it, simply photocopy your application if you need more copies (ie, as a worksheet). For detailed advice on completing the Universal Application, see Chapter 5.

B Program Designation and Acknowledgment Card

This self-addressed card to acknowledge receipt of your application is a bit lame; it has no space for the program secretary to acknowledge receipt of other materials for your dossier, such as letters of recommendation and medical school transcripts. You can easily design a more useful acknowledgment card yourself (see "Application Complete Postcard," pg. 82). One free card comes with your Universal Application.

TABLE 1–4. Must-see tables/charts.	
Tables/Charts	**What to Look For**
Applicants in the Matching program	Detailed Match statistics, grouped by applicant category. Compares U.S. seniors to foreign graduates.
PGY-1 positions, active applicants, and Match rates	Presents similar information as previous table, but in the context of the number of PGY-1 positions available.
Positions offered and % filled by U.S. seniors and total applicants	Breaks down Match fill rates over the previous 5 years by specialty. Allows you to spot trends in each specialty.
Programs, positions, ranked and filled	The rank/position value is the average number of times each position offered by that specialty was ranked. A rank/position value roughly corresponds to the degree of competitiveness—the higher the number, the tougher it is to get the spot.
U.S. seniors unmatched	Highlights the specialties in which students have had the most difficulty matching.

REFERENCES

Graettinger JS, Peranson E: The matching program. *N Engl J Med* 1981;304:1163.
National Residency Matching Program, *NRMP Data: March 1995*. Washington, DC, 1995.

Setting Up the Fourth Year

HOW DO I PICK AN ADVISER?

During your first 3 years of medical school, you might have been graced with an academic adviser who shepherded you through a variety of situations, from surviving gross anatomy to helping you choose a medical specialty. If your adviser is an internist and you want to go into internal medicine, you might already be in great shape. However, if you choose a field different from that of your adviser or if your adviser does not monitor your application and matching process, then you definitely need a second adviser for career purposes to provide you with additional direction and advocacy.

In selecting an adviser, you want someone who is savvy about a wide variety of factors regarding your career choice and the Match (Figure 2–1). Your adviser should be able to keep you informed of both academic and economic trends as well as training and job opportunities in your chosen field. Find an adviser who is familiar with the programs in which you are interested. For example, an adviser who trained on the East Coast may not be familiar with the West Coast programs. Your adviser should also be able to answer a range of questions about the application process, from matters of fact (When are the deadlines?) to advice (Whom should I ask for recommendations?).

Some students recommend a dual-adviser system: one adviser to assist you with the "nuts and bolts" of the process and a more senior, well-known faculty member whose connections and telephone lobbying might open more doors for you.

How do you find such adviser? Start by asking students in the class ahead of you about outstanding members of your field. Your current medical school adviser may also know of the same people. Desirable advisers are usually junior or senior faculty currently on the residency selection committee. In trying for the ideal adviser, be aware of the following potential pitfalls:

ADVISERS SHOULD SERVE AS BOTH COUNSELOR AND ADVOCATE.

FIGURE 2-1

☐ Discuss current academic and economic trends in the field
☐ Point out research opportunities
☐ Provide overall view of the application process
☐ Offer honest assessment of your competitive standing
☐ Highlight programs most appropriate for you
☐ Review and critique your application (eg, personal statement, CV)
☐ Conduct a mock interview
☐ Review your rank-order list
☐ Make key "political" phone calls if necessary
☐ Be available on Unmatch Day

Checklist for the career adviser.

- **Adviser overload:** The person is counseling so many students that you're left with little attention
- **Adviser oversight:** He or she tends to misjudge a student's competitiveness or the competitiveness of the field
- **Adviser bias:** One who gives all students the same "pet" list of programs to apply to regardless of their personal career goals or geographic constraints

WHEN SHOULD I SCHEDULE MY ACTING INTERNSHIPS?

Figure 2–2 offers a checklist/time line for organizing Match activities during your fourth year in medical school. Conventional wisdom says that you should do at least one acting internship (AI; aka subinternship, externship, junior internship, or senior clerkship) in your target specialty early in your fourth year. Your evaluation during this rotation is one of the most influential factors considered by the selection committee. In addition, a strong letter of recommendation from an attending physician on this rotation is usually key to a competitive application. Verify with the dean's office the last rotation block that will show up in your dean's letter and on your transcript (usually September).

Because of the importance of this rotation, many students like to take a "warm-up" rotation before going all out on the AI. For example, students interested in internal medicine often take cardiology, infectious disease, or an emergency medicine rotation before the internal medicine AI. The warm-up rotation allows you to acquire the experience, knowledge, and skills (political and manual) that are necessary for success on your AI. The warm-up rotation also ensures that you enter the AI refreshed and enthusiastic. However, don't relax too much; strong grades or evaluations in electives of your target specialty are also highly prized by the selection committee.

If you do other AIs, either by requirement or by desire, note that there are good reasons for doing them early and for postponing them (Table 2–1).

KEEP IN MIND THE LAST SENIOR BLOCK THAT WILL APPEAR IN YOUR DEAN'S LETTER.

SCHEDULE THE AI AFTER YOUR SUMMER BREAK OR A LIGHT "WARM-UP" ROTATION.

FIGURE 2-2

Task	Page	Mar	Apr	May	June	July	Aug	Sep	Oct	Nov	Dec	Jan	Feb	Mar	Apr	May
☐ Choose/meet with career adviser	11	├─	—	—	─┤											
☐ Plan senior year—subls, electives, audition rotations, etc.	12	├─	—	─┤												
☐ Enroll in Match	55		├─	─┤												
☐ Request program applications	60				├─	─┤										
☐ Request letters of recommendation	79				├─	─┤										
☐ Create CV	85			├─	—	─┤										
☐ Create personal statement	97				├─	─┤										
☐ Buy interview clothes	124						├─	─┤								
☐ Take application photos	81						├─┤									
☐ Review/request dean's letter and transcripts	77							├─	─┤							
☐ Mail application materials	71							├─	─┤							
☐ Schedule interviews/follow-up applications	121								├─	─┤						
☐ Interview at programs	135									├─	—	─┤				
☐ Write follow-up letters	143										├─	─┤				
☐ Create/submit rank lists	145												├─┤			
☐ Thank adviser and letter writers	151													├┤		
☐ Send in *First Aid for the Match* surveys	158													├─	─┤	
☐ Sign residency contract	152														├─	─┤

Match Day!

First Aid for the NRMP Match time line.

TABLE 2–1. Deciding when to do your second AI.
Advantages of Doing Second AI Early
• Offers another chance for a strong letter of recommendation (especially if third-year performance was weak) • Strong evaluation on Dean's letter a major plus • Allows for a cushy spring schedule
Advantages of Doing Second AI Late
• Evaluation won't be included in Dean's letter; more freedom to dictate learning objectives • Tough rotations are distributed more evenly in fourth year; prevents burnout

WHEN SHOULD I SCHEDULE INTERVIEW TIME?

For the majority of students, interview dates run from November to early February. Most students take a month off for interviews, starting right before or after Christmas break. Unless you are considering programs in a limited area or in numbers, a 2-week Christmas break is usually not enough time.

Students who interview in January may have a slight advantage over those who interview earlier. Because their interviews occur after the holidays, committee members more readily remember the specifics of their applications and can really push for them during highly charged ranking sessions.

However, if you plan to hit many programs in the Northeast or upper Midwest, January may be a bad month because of winter traveling conditions. During the first week of January, one of us got stranded at a subway stop in a blizzard while visiting a program in Cleveland. A half-hour trip from the airport to the university turned into a two-and-a-half-hour ordeal. So allow extra time during snow season for visiting programs in these areas.

SHOULD I STICK AROUND MY SCHOOL ON MATCH DAY?

The month featuring Match Day (March for most applicants) is generally not a good time to be vacationing or doing electives outside the country. If you feel the need to flee, choose another time. A certain percentage of U.S. medical students and international medical graduates will not be placed on Match Day and will have to enter the Scramble. If you do not match and have to enter the Scramble or if there is a problem with your rank list, you'll need to be in close communication with your dean and your adviser, either in person or by phone. This is especially true if you are trying to match in a competitive specialty. If you must be out of the country, make contingency plans with your dean and adviser, and find access to a fax machine.

SHOULD I DO AUDITION ROTATIONS?

Early in the fourth year, many students do audition rotations (aka away rotations or externships) at other schools in their target specialties to find out

PLAY IT SAFE. BE IN THE COUNTRY AROUND MATCH DAY.

more about a specific program or to improve their chances of entering that program. Be careful. An away rotation is a two-edged sword—you can stumble as well as shine. Remember that you will probably be compared with medical students at that institution who are already familiar with the hospital environment and its faculty.

On the positive side, many programs will grant visiting students a "courtesy interview" at the end of an audition rotation. In fact, some programs in certain very competitive specialties, such as orthopedic surgery or emergency medicine, only take "known quantities"—students who have done rotations on site.

For the rest of you, consider doing away rotations only if you are aiming for a long-shot program in which you would not otherwise have a chance. In evaluating the potential benefits of an audition rotation, you must size up whether you come across better in person or on paper. If you simply want to find out more about a program at a specific institution, consider doing an away rotation there but not in your target specialty (eg, emergency medicine at an institution whose surgery program interests you). Otherwise, you risk exposing yourself to unnecessary scrutiny.

WHAT ABOUT OTHER ELECTIVES?

Your fourth year is a fantastic opportunity to fulfill your intellectual and personal curiosity by sampling all that medicine has to offer. Don't waste it! Though it's wise to take an elective or two that will prepare you for internship, do not try to duplicate your internship during your fourth year: You'll get more than enough experience during your residency training. In addition, you might enjoy taking some electives that might not be available to you ever again (Table 2–2). Your career adviser should have some good suggestions for fourth-year electives, as will students in the class ahead of you.

WHEN SHOULD I SCHEDULE VACATION?

Don't forget to take a little time for yourself. Some students take a light rotation during September of their fourth year or take 2 weeks off during that period so that they can take care of residency applications. Remember that once residency starts, you will be limited to only 3 to 5 weeks of vacation per year—and you can probably forget holidays such as Christmas, Hanukkah, and Thanksgiving.

Consider spending part of your vacation at a major national meeting in one or two of your top specialty choices late in your third year or early in your fourth year, especially if the meeting is nearby or if your adviser is planning to go (Table 2–3). A list of national meetings is published regularly in the *Journal of the American Medical Association*. Most of these conferences have special reduced registration rates for medical students. Your career adviser can provide more detailed information about the best ones to attend. At these meetings, you can meet the field's celebrities, find out what's hot, hear about problems and politics, scope out the turf wars, etc. You can preview programs in the specialty by looking for their research posters or by listening to some of their scheduled faculty talks. Spending time at a major meeting will provide you with valuable insights and perspectives and can also make you a more knowledgeable and interesting candidate during interviews.

AUDITION ROTATIONS CAN HURT AS MUCH AS THEY HELP.

FULFILL YOUR LEARNING DESIRES WITHOUT DUPLICATING YOUR INTERNSHIP.

ATTEND A MAJOR NATIONAL MEETING IN YOUR DESIRED SPECIALTY.

Specialty	Recommended Electives for Internship	Related Electives
Anesthesiology	Surgical ICU	Radiology, emergency medicine, medical ethics
Dermatology	Infectious disease, medicine subinternship, pathology	Emergency medicine, ophthalmology, radiology
Emergency medicine	ICU, radiology, gynecology	Cardiology, dermatology, psychiatry crisis center
Family practice	Cardiology, emergency medicine, gastroenterology, orthopedics	Dermatology, ophthalmology, overseas elective, radiology, sports medicine
Internal medicine	Cardiology, emergency medicine, infectious disease, pulmonary	Dermatology, orthopedics, OB/GYN, otolaryngology, overseas elective
Neurology	Psychiatry subinternship, radiology	Neurosurgery
Obstetrics & gynecology	Maternal/fetal medicine, pediatrics	Emergency medicine, family practice, endocrinology
Orthopedics	Emergency medicine, trauma surgery	ICU, medicine consult, radiology
Otolaryngology	Emergency medicine, neurology	Dermatology, pulmonary medicine
Ophthalmology	Emergency medicine, neurology	Dermatology, medicine consult
Pathology	Clinical anatomy, radiology	Laboratory medicine
Pediatrics	Emergency medicine, dermatology, pediatric infectious disease, pediatric intensive care medicine	Child psychiatry, medicine consult, radiology
Psychiatry	Endocrinology, neurology subinternship	Emergency medicine, toxicology, substance abuse
Radiology	Clinical anatomy, anatomic pathology	Informatics, orthopedics, emergency medicine
Surgery	Emergency medicine, ICU, trauma surgery, clinical anatomy	Medicine consult, anatomic pathology

TABLE 2–2. Recommended fourth-year electives by specialty.

TABLE 2–3. Partial list of national meetings in 1996 and 1997.			
Specialty	**Organization/Contact Number**	**Location/Dates 1996**	**Location/Dates 1997**
General	American Medical Women's Association 703-838-0500	Boston, MA Oct. 29–Nov. 3	***TBA***
	American Medical Association 312-464-4742	Chicago, IL June 23–27 Atlanta, GA December 8–11	Chicago, IL June 22–26
	American Medical Student Association 703-620-6600	Washington, DC March 14–17	Orlando, FL March 19–23
Anesthesiology	American Society of Anesthesiologists 708-825-5586	New Orleans, LA October 19–23	San Diego, CA October 18–22
Dermatology	American Academy of Dermatology 708-330-0230	Washington, DC February 10–15	San Francisco, CA March 21–26
Emergency medicine	National Association of EMS Physicians 412-578-3222 or 800-228-3677	Naples, FL January 11–14	Naples, FL January 9–14
	American College of Emergency Physicians 214-550-0911 or 800-798-1822	Calendar of meetings available from ACEP	
Family practice	American Academy of Family Physicians 816-333-9700	Kansas City, MO August 1–4	Kansas City, MO July 31–Aug. 3
Internal medicine	American College of Physicians 800-523-1546	San Francisco April 25–28	Philadelphia, PA March 22–25
	American College of Cardiology 301-897-5400	Orlando, FL March 24–27	Anaheim, CA March 16–19
Neurology	American Academy of Neurology 404-778-4369	San Francisco, CA March 23–30	Boston, MA April 12–19
	American Neurological Association 612-623-2401	Miami, FL October 13–16	San Diego, CA Sept. 28–Oct. 1
Neurosurgery	Congress of Neurological Surgeons 404-778-4369	Montreal, Quebec Sept. 28–Oct. 3	New Orleans, LA Sept. 27–Oct. 2
	American Association of Neurological Surgeons 708-692-9500	Minneapolis, MN April 27–May 2	Denver, CO April 12–17
Obstetrics & gynecology	American Gynecological and Obstetrical Society 206-543-3580	Asheville, NC September 5–7	Victoria, BC September 5–7
Ophthalmology	American Academy of Ophthalmology 415-561-8500	Chicago, IL October 27–31	San Francisco, CA October 26–30
Orthopedics	American Academy of Orthopedic Surgeons 708-823-7186	Atlanta, GA February 22–26	San Francisco, CA February 13–17
Pathology	American Society of Clinical Pathologists 312-738-1336	Boston, MA April 20–25 San Diego, CA Sept. 28–Oct. 4	Chicago, IL April 5–10 Philadelphia, PA September 20–26
	College of American Pathologists 708-446-8800	Same as ASCP above	Same as ASCP above
	U.S. and Canadian Academy of Pathology 706-733-7550	Washington, DC March 23–29	Orlando, FL March 1–7
Pediatrics	American Academy of Pediatrics 708-228-5005	Boston, MA October 26–30	New Orleans, LA November 1–5

Specialty	Organization/Contact Number	Location/Dates 1996	Location/Dates 1997
Psychiatry	American Academy of Clinical Psychiatrists 619-298-0538	Ft. Lauderdale, FL October 10–12	New Orleans, LA October 8–10
	American Psychiatric Association	New York, NY May 4–9	San Diego, CA May 17–22
Radiology	American College of Radiology 703-648-8900	Calendar of meetings available from ACR	
	Radiology Society of North America	Chicago, IL December 1–6	Chicago, IL November 30–Dec 5
Surgery	American College of Surgeons 312-664-4050	San Francisco, CA October 6–11	Chicago, IL October 12–17

TABLE 2–3. Partial list of national meetings in 1996 and 1997. (Continued)

REFERENCES

Reference directories. *JAMA* 1995;273(21):1652.

Wagoner NE, Suriano R, Stoner JA: Factors used by program directors to select residents. *J Med Educ* 1986;61:10.

Your Specialty and the Match

In Chapter 1, you were introduced to several different matches. It's not surprising that each match has its own set of rules and strategies for success. But even within the NRMP Match, each specialty calls for a different approach to preparing a successful application and interview. For example, psychiatry residency directors expect and appreciate in-depth personal statements with thorough exploration of an applicant's background and motives for entering the specialty. A surgery residency director, on the other hand, might toss the same statement out the window in disgust. In that director's opinion, personal statements ought to be as succinct as possible.

In this chapter, we briefly profile selected specialties (see Table 3–1 for factors considered by medical students in choosing a specialty). Some of the smaller specialties are not profiled here. We have organized the information and advice for each specialty under the following headings:

Overview: The specialty in terms of recent trends in the medical career market.

Match Numbers: An analysis of recent Match results.

Application Tips: Advice and guidance for the application process specific for that specialty.

Interview Tips: Advice and guidance for the interview visit specific to that specialty.

For More Info . . . : A collection of essential career and residency application resources for the specialty.

The **Overview,** a brief description of the specialty itself as well as a glance at its socioeconomic trends, summarizes student, resident, and faculty observations. It is **not** intended as a basis for the complex and critical process of specialty selection. For more in-depth information about the specialty, consult the following resources:

► Faculty and house staff in the field
► Brochures from the academic or certifying society in the field (listed under "For More Info . . . .")
► Glaxo Wellcome Pathway Evaluation Program. This is a free half-day seminar sometimes offered by the dean's office that helps you match your interests to different specialties. These seminars feature the *Glaxo*

DIFFERENT STROKES FOR DIFFERENT FOLKS.

TABLE 3–1. Most influential factors determining specialty choice.

Type and range of patient problems encountered
Appropriateness for personality
Opportunity to make a difference in people's lives
Desire to help people
Intellectual appeal of the specialty
The challenge of diagnostic problems
Diversity of diagnosis and therapy

Medical Specialties Survey (1991), a catalog of medical specialties and subspecialties complete with descriptions, practitioner profiles, and anecdotal picks and pans. Contact your student affairs office for details.

► Taylor A.: *How to Choose a Medical Specialty*, 2nd ed. Philadelphia: Saunders, 1993. This resource contains detailed descriptions of most medical specialties, together with work sheets and exercises that allow you to find specialties compatible with your interests.

ANESTHESIOLOGY

Factors attracting students to careers in anesthesiology include brief but positive doctor/patient relationships, above-average income, immediate results, and a more flexible lifestyle than other specialties. However, the field of anesthesiology has reached saturation, especially in major urban centers. Even outside big cities, many graduating anesthesiologists report difficulty finding employment. As more responsibilities are shifted to nurse anesthetists, graduating anesthesiologists will continue to see job prospects shrink, workloads increase, and income drop (Figure 3–1C). On the other hand, opportunities for entering post-residency fellowship training in such areas as critical care, pain management, and respiratory care have increased in recent years.

All anesthesiology residencies require a prior internship year, followed by 3 years of training in anesthesiology. The internship requirement can be satisfied by a preliminary medicine, surgery, or transitional program. The bulk of training time will be spent in operating rooms and inpatient wards. The resident will learn the techniques of care for both stable and high-risk populations, as well as learn about basic medical illnesses and critical care issues.

Match Numbers

Given the employment challenges facing graduating anesthesiologists, it's no surprise that the bottom fell out of the National Residency Matching Program (NRMP) anesthesiology match. Several prestigious programs were not filled on Match Day and had to enter the Scramble. There were 324 (Post-Graduate Year) PGY-1 and PGY-2 positions filled from the 960 available, down from 825 positions filled last year (Figure 3–1A). Despite a cut in over 450 anesthesiology positions since the 1993 Match, the fill rate fell to 34%, down from 66.5% over the past 3 years (Figure 3–1B). In the same period, the number of U.S. senior medical students entering anesthesiology plummeted by two-thirds. Expect future reductions in anesthesiology positions in response to the decreasing popularity of the specialty.

Application Tips

With decreasing medical student interest in the specialty, the anesthesiology match is definitely a buyer's market. Most prestigious programs emphasize good clinical grades and strong letters of evaluation—especially from the anesthesiology attending physician or head of the anesthesiology department—over board scores. Indeed, a recent study (based on data collected when anesthesiology was more competitive) demonstrated that only higher scores for letters of recommendation and interviews differentiated those that matched in anesthesiology from the applicant pool at large. All application material should be submitted by October. For the average to above-average student, advisers suggest that 10 to 15 applications are sufficient to get a comfortable 8 to 10 interviews. Plan to coordinate separate applications and interviews for internship positions. Often, hospitals can arrange interviews for internship and anesthesiology positions on the same day, so be sure to ask about this possibility when scheduling interviews.

FIGURES 3–1A–C

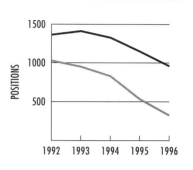

— POSITIONS OFFERED
— POSITIONS FILLED

Positions offered in anesthesiology and number filled.

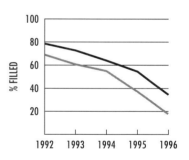

— TOTAL % FILLED
— U.S. % FILLED

Percentage of anesthesiology positions filled on Match Day.

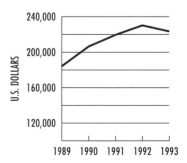

Mean income of anesthesiologists in U.S. dollars.

Interview Tips

Typically, interview days begin at 8 AM and end early in the afternoon. Most interviews last 30 to 60 minutes, followed by a tour of the hospital and opportunities to speak with house staff. There are usually no difficult questions or pimping, but you may be asked your views of the specialty's future, including the decreasing job opportunities. Be prepared to discuss your ability to be a team player and work with other physicians, especially surgeons.

For More Info . . .

▶ *American Society of Anesthesiologists Information Packet.* This free career information packet includes general articles (of marginal value) on the specialty itself, a directory of anesthesiology training programs as listed in the *Graduate Medical Education Directory*, and a directory of fellowships for specialized training in pain management. The packet can be obtained by contacting:

American Society of Anesthesiologists
520 North Northwest Highway
Park Ridge, IL 60068
(708) 825-5586

DERMATOLOGY

In general, established dermatologists enjoy good working hours, high income levels, a variety of procedures, and a typically healthy patient population. However, the field suffers from a poor distribution of physicians. There are openings available in smaller communities and rural areas, whereas most urban centers are saturated. With increasing emphasis on primary care, practicing dermatologists face cutbacks in their range and amount of work. The relatively routine and milder skin diseases are increasingly being treated by primary care physicians. As a result, more attention is being paid to the diagnosis of oncologic diseases, surgical procedures, and cosmetic treatments not covered by managed care contracts.

Specialty training in dermatology requires 1 year of internship, followed by 3 years of residency. A preliminary medicine year is preferable, but any training involving clinical patient care, such as surgery or transitional medicine, is usually acceptable. Residency training will include diagnostic and therapeutic procedures, both medical and surgical, with emphasis varying according to the particular program.

Match Numbers

Dermatology continues to be one of the most difficult specialties to match. In October 1994, 34% of U.S. seniors who applied in dermatology failed to match. However, because of the saturated job market, programs will attempt to reduce the number of positions offered. Many are aiming for a reduction in total spots of at least 10% in the coming year (Figure 3–2A). Because of this trend, dermatology will remain one of the most competitive specialties, with 100% of positions filled (Figure 3–2B).

Application Tips

The NRMP-run dermatology match has traditionally been a late match run in October of the applicant's internship year. Because of the late match, your selection committees could evaluate your late fall rotations as well as your internship plans. In 1997, the dermatology match will take place in March with the rest of the NRMP Match. As a result, your Dean's letter will not have your late fall grades and the selection committees will have no idea that you lined up a cushy preliminary year in Hawaii. However, that does not make dermatology any easier to enter.

Dermatology programs screen applicants intensively before offering interviews to prospective residents. Many use AΩA status, at least three honors in clinical rotations, high board scores, and a top-notch dean's letter as preliminary considerations. A glowing evaluation in the dermatology subinternship and supportive letters of recommendation are vital. However, given the competitive nature of the specialty, applicants need to demonstrate more than just academic excellence. Most dermatology programs also want proof of your undying loyalty to the specialty and your ability to contribute to the field after finishing your training. Consequently, political connections within dermatology circles as well as long-term research or clinical projects in the field serve to build a strong application. Since the total number of spots offered is small, applicants generally apply to 12 or more programs to increase

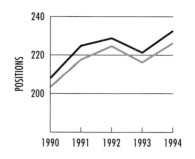

POSITIONS OFFERED
POSITIONS FILLED

Positions offered in dermatology and number filled.

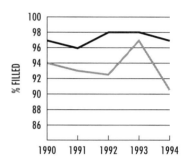

TOTAL % FILLED
U.S. % FILLED

Percentage of dermatology positions filled on Match Day.

A TRACK RECORD
IN DERMATOLOGY RESEARCH
IS CONSIDERED A BIG PLUS.

FIGURE 3-2C

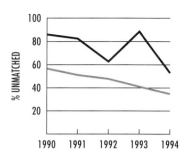

Percentage of applicants unmatched in dermatology on Match Day.

their chance of success. Consider registering for the regular NRMP Match in case you are unable to match in dermatology.

Interview Tips

Since there are many stellar applicants in this small field, the interview is often a heavily weighted factor for acceptance. Though the majority of programs wrap up their interviews in June, many still conduct interviews as late as August, disrupting the first few months of the applicant's internship. Dermatology programs usually offer interviews to about only 10 to 15% of their applicants. They may offer three to six interviews per day, lasting 30 to 45 minutes each. Depending on the program, interviews may be conducted by individual faculty members or by a panel consisting of three or more interviewers. Interviews are designed to measure the applicant's interest in the specialty and to evaluate his or her potential for contribution in the future, as well as to find out whether he or she would get along with other people in the department. The applicant is rarely pimped, but will be expected to discuss any prior research or involvement in dermatology intelligently and in detail.

For More Info . . .

▶ *American Academy of Dermatology Information Packet.* This free information packet includes a mind-numbing description of accredited dermatology training programs and a list of dermatology programs worldwide as well as of dermatology fellowships in North America. The packet can be obtained by contacting:

American Academy of Dermatology
930 North Meacham Road
Schaumberg, IL 60173-4965
(708) 330-0230, ext 365

EMERGENCY MEDICINE

Emergency medicine (EM) has enjoyed tremendous growth over the past few years, with good reason. Regular working hours, relatively abundant free time, and the ability to integrate medicine with surgical procedures all add to this field's appeal. This is also one of the few specialties in which one can become an attending straight out of residency training. Moreover, post-residency fellowships are plentiful and easily obtained for those desiring further training. EM physicians enjoy versatility and flexibility in pursuing such exotic fields as international health, disaster/rescue medicine, and diving medicine. And now with the television show "ER," it's a glamorous specialty to boot. Unfortunately, EM is infamous for a high burnout rate, attributable to high-stress working conditions, hostile patients, and the possibility of never-ending night shifts for junior attendings.

Residency programs in emergency medicine require either 3 or 4 years total training. In either case, the internship year is usually integrated with the main EM training. For the non-integrated programs, a separate internship year can be done in the field of medicine, surgery, or transitional medicine. The bulk of EM training time is spent in emergency rooms, learning resuscitation techniques, and treating both medical and trauma-related illnesses. However, residents will also rotate through specialties such as medicine, pediatrics, OB/GYN, surgery, anesthesiology, and orthopedic surgery to acquire a well-rounded knowledge and to develop an eye for common emergencies in these fields.

Match Numbers

Competition for spots in emergency medicine residencies continues to intensify, despite the addition of 117 positions to the 1996 Match. In 1996, 1017 positions were filled from the 1030 offered through the Match (99% fill rate) (Figure 3–3A, Figure 3–3B). This high fill rate marks an upward trend in the number of applicants to the field, as EM residencies become increasingly competitive. In fact, 13% of all U.S. seniors who applied in emergency medicine failed to match and had to scramble.

Application Tips

Given the competitive nature of EM, all aspects of the residency application are important. It is especially critical to do well in an EM rotation and to ask for strong letters of recommendation from the attending physicians or the chief of emergency medicine. Letters from surgery, medicine, pediatrics, or OB/GYN are also well regarded. Competitive programs often use the USMLE Step 1 score to screen applications. To improve your chances with a very competitive program, consider doing an externship at that institution, especially if you are not particularly strong on paper (if you do the externship, prepare to excel). All application and supporting material, except for the dean's letter, should be submitted by early October. The optimal number of applications to submit depends on the candidate's strength, but many suggest 15 to 20 applications to yield 10 to 12 interviews.

Interview Tips

Expect three to four interview sessions, typically lasting 30 to 60 minutes in length and conducted by the residency directors, attendings, and residents, as well as ER nurses and technicians. In general, interviewers are relaxed,

"ER" SHOW PET PEEVES: (1) NOBODY DOES A C-SECTION IN THE ER. (2) PLACE IS WAY TOO CLEAN. (3) PATIENTS ARE WAY TOO NICE. (4) HOW COME MED STUDENT GETS TO INTUBATE RIGHT AND LEFT?

FIGURES 3–3A–B

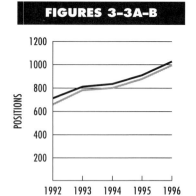

— POSITIONS OFFERED
— POSITIONS FILLED

Positions offered in emergency medicine and number filled.

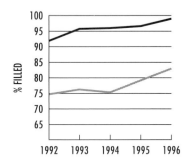

— TOTAL % FILLED
— U.S. % FILLED

Percentage of emergency medicine positions filled on Match Day.

friendly, and genuinely interested both in giving information about the programs and learning more about the applicant's personality.

For More Info . . .

▶ **ACEP Student Information Packet.** The packet includes a directory of emergency medicine training programs. To obtain a copy, write or call:

American College of Emergency Physicians
P.O. Box 619911
Dallas, TX 75261-9911
(214) 550-0911
(800) 798-1822

▶ Emergency Medicine Residents' Association (EMRA). In addition to the general information packet, you may wish to take out a student membership in the EMRA. A $45 annual fee provides you with a subscription to *Annals of Emergency Medicine*; *ACEP News*, a monthly newsletter; *EM Resident*, a bimonthly newsletter; and access to specialty meetings and conferences. Since the medical student affiliate (MSA) branch of EMRA was created in 1992, most information remains geared toward residents. To enroll, call:

Emergency Medicine Residents' Association
(800) 798-1822

For further reading:

▶ Delbridge, TR. *Emergency Medicine In Focus: A Handbook for Medical Students and Prospective Residents*. A compact guide to the emergency medicine residency application process and, it is available to EMRA/ MSA members for $15. To order, call:

ACEP Publications
(800) 798-1822, touch 6

▶ Koscove, EM: An applicant's evaluation of an emergency medicine internship and residency. *Ann Emerg Med* 1990;19:774. This article offers an exhaustive collection of factors to consider when applying and interviewing at emergency medicine training programs.

FAMILY PRACTICE

Family practice (aka family medicine or family and community medicine) embraces the biopsychosocial model in its treatment of individuals and of the family as a whole. Students entering family practice have a strong commitment to primary care and enjoy the wide variety of patients and clinical problems encountered in this specialty, which spans medicine, pediatrics, OB/GYN, and surgery. Do not make the *faux pas* of calling this specialty *general practice*, as this term refers to the general practitioner (GP) of old who practiced general medicine immediately after internship. In today's world, an inexperienced GP can wave goodbye to good jobs in competitive locations.

Family practice graduates who are willing to practice medicine outside academic settings enjoy bright job prospects throughout the country, thanks especially to the growing presence of managed care. In an academic center, the family practice graduate can be an attending physician right out of residency. Though subspecialty opportunities are limited, sports medicine, geriatrics, and adolescent medicine are booming growth areas and very popular among residents. Finally, there is growing opportunity for fellowship training in academic subjects, which, for family practice, often focuses on epidemiology and public health.

In family practice, there is no consensus about the "best" programs. You can identify only the most "popular" programs, which depend on geographic region—university versus community versus rural. Note that curricula vary with geography, especially in the amount of obstetrics taught. The most formal training and education are afforded by a university setting; however, family practice here often gets trampled by internal medicine. Community-based programs usually have the run of the hospital; however, specialty training and didactic teaching often suffer. Rural-based programs are not as numerous as the others. Residents usually learn practical clinical skills and low-tech medicine in a non-academic, preceptorship-like atmosphere. The Midwest and the West Coast generally have a more favorable orientation toward family practice.

If your school does not have a family practice department, you will probably have to hustle to put together a strong application. Possible obstacles: lack of solid career guidance and no clinical experience to buttress your reasons for going into family practice. Plan to take extra steps to arrange a family practice preceptorship.

Match Numbers

Over the past several years, family practice has enjoyed a renaissance (Figure 3–4C). In 1996, family practice led the primary care charge with an all-time high of 2,840 positions filled, up 280 spots from the previous year (Figure 3–4A). A record 16.1% of U.S. seniors went into family practice, allowing the specialty to fill over 90.5% of its available positions (Figure 3–4B).

Application Tips

Given the rising interest in family practice, some applicants are now finding that matching up with a good program is no longer a sure thing. In applying, keep the following considerations in mind. Programs want to see a strong commitment to family medicine. They favor experience in public health, as well as evidence of a mature, well-rounded personality. In addition, programs are more sensitive to your reasons for choosing family practice over internal medicine (especially primary care internal medicine). Program directors like

FIGURES 3-4A-B

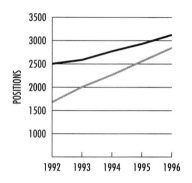

— POSITIONS OFFERED
— POSITIONS FILLED

Positions offered in family practice and number filled.

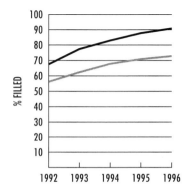

— TOTAL % FILLED
— U.S. % FILLED

Percentage of family practice positions filled on Match Day.

"EACH YEAR WE SEE APPLICANTS WHO ARE UNABLE TO REALLY TELL US WHY THEY WANT TO GO INTO FAMILY PRACTICE BECAUSE THEY DIDN'T HAVE ADEQUATE EXPERIENCE IN THE FIELD."
—*FAMILY PRACTICE RESIDENCY DIRECTOR*

FIGURE 3-4C

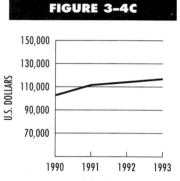

Mean income of family practitioners in U.S. dollars.

to see a demonstrated interest in OB/GYN and pediatrics. Given the varying foci of different programs, you may consider customizing your personal statement to best address the training philosophies of each program or at least each type of program (university vs community vs rural). Like other primary care specialties, family practice residencies will scrutinize your personal statement very carefully. Indeed, aside from the interview, family practice residency directors in a recent study singled out the Dean's letter, the personal statement, and transcripts as the most useful selection criteria.

Mail your applications no later than mid-October. Many programs actually grant interviews on a first-come, first-served basis. Submit as many applications as you wish. Students recommend interviewing at a minimum of six programs, with eight to ten being a more comfortable range.

Interview Tips

Because family practice programs tend to be smaller, the visit (generally with two to four interviews) tends toward the personal. Prepare for "touchy-feely" type questions. Are you concerned with the human side of medicine? What do you want to do with your training in family practice? Work overseas for a few years? Do rural medicine? Focus on women's health? Think through these and similar questions. Reading up on social and ethical issues in medicine may help broaden your perspective and get you psyched for the interviews.

For More Info . . .

▶ American Academy of Family Physicians
8880 Ward Parkway
Kansas City, MO 64114
(800) 274-2237, ext. 5224 or
(816) 333-9700, ext. 5224

▶ **AAFP Student Membership.** For a mere $10 per year, you will receive a subscription to the journal *American Family Physician*, which features practical articles on family medicine topics; the newsweekly *AAFP Reporter*; and a directory of family practice clerkships/preceptorships for students desiring clinical experience in family practice. Membership is limited to medical students at LCME accredited medical schools. To enroll, contact:

AAFP Membership Records
(800) 274-2237

▶ **AAFP Publications.** The AAFP has a number of publications, many complimentary, aimed at medical students considering family practice:

▶ *Directory of Family Practice Residency Programs.* This is an annually revised database of family practice residencies, considered more accurate, more informative and more up-to-date than either FREIDA or the "Green Book." It is free to medical students through your school's family medicine department. Otherwise, the cost per copy is $10 for members, $15 for non-members.

▶ *Reprint 300.* This booklet contains definitions of family practice and family physicians; free on request.

▶ *Facts About Family Practice.* For number-crunchers, this book includes detailed statistics about family practice. Cost: $25 for members/$40 for non-members.

To order, call:

AAFP Order Department
(800) 274-2237

▶ Scherger JE et al: Responses to questions about family practice as a career. *Am Fam Physician* 1992;46(1):115. This article presents responses to 20 common questions about family practice; it is informative but reads like thinly veiled propaganda.

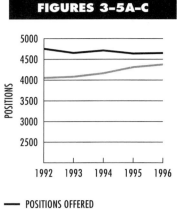

POSITIONS

1992 1993 1994 1995 1996

— POSITIONS OFFERED
— POSITIONS FILLED

Positions offered in internal medicine and number filled.

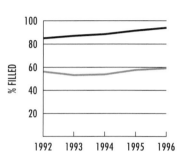

% FILLED

1992 1993 1994 1995 1996

— TOTAL % FILLED
— U.S. % FILLED

Percentage of internal medicine positions filled on Match Day.

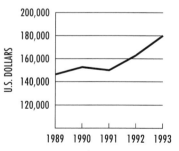

U.S. DOLLARS

1989 1990 1991 1992 1993

Mean income of internists in U.S. dollars.

INTERNAL MEDICINE

Internal medicine programs are usually divided into "traditional" programs and primary care programs. Traditional medicine offers more of an inpatient focus, plus electives for sampling different subspecialties. Residents in primary care medicine have more of an outpatient experience and often receive additional training in gynecology and pediatrics. Students are often attracted to traditional internal medicine because it leaves the door open for further subspecialty training or generalist practice. On the other hand, students going into primary care internal medicine are often committed to primary care but are not as interested in the obstetrics, pediatrics and surgical assisting experience offered by family practice. Primary care internal medicine programs maintain that their graduates are better suited to enter community practice than are their traditional counterparts.

Many students are attracted to general internal medicine because of its emphasis on adult care, complex problem-solving, and continuity of care. Practical advantages include broadening job prospects for general internists, especially in managed care settings, and the flexibility to go into primary care or pursue subspecialty training. However, medicine subspecialists are currently facing an oversupply of subspecialists, bread and butter procedures lost to primary care physicians, and shrinking reimbursement schedules from Medicare and managed care plans.

Match Numbers

In 1996, 4654 traditional positions were offered through the Match. On Match Day 1995, a record-high 94% of those positions were filled by 4282 applicants, continuing the trend toward rising fill rates (Figure 3–5A). This trend is mirrored by primary care internal medicine and medicine-pediatrics. Compared with family medicine, in which 73% of available positions were filled by U.S. graduates, one-third of the available internal medicine positions were filled by international medical graduates (Figure 3–5B).

Application Tips

The best thing you can do for your internal medicine application is to pull down strong evaluations in your junior and senior medicine clerkships, as well as enthused letters of recommendations. Primary care programs place a bit more emphasis on the applicant's personal goals, skills, interests, and career plans in general internal medicine. Most competitive residency programs, including several of the most prestigious, couldn't care less about Step 1 scores as long as you passed. Externships are not the norm, unless you want to try to improve your chances at an otherwise long-shot program. Plan to submit all your residency applications and supporting material by the beginning of October; ignore those February application deadlines. Again, there are no hard and fast rules about the number of applications you should complete; however, some residency advisers suggest that the typical student send in 10 to 15 applications in order to secure interviews at 8 to 10 programs.

Interview Tips

The typical interview day starts at 8 AM and goes to about 3 PM. Applicants usually receive two or three 20- or 30-minute interviews. In general, internal medicine programs conduct interviews in a relatively benign fashion; however, that does not mean that you can drop your guard. Be prepared for tough questions concerning personal strengths and weaknesses, medical ethics, or clinical scenarios.

For more info . . .

▶ American College of Physicians
Independence Mall West
Sixth Street at Race
Philadelphia, PA 19106-1572
(800) 523-1546

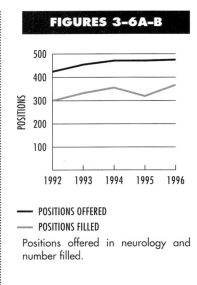

FIGURES 3–6A–B

POSITIONS OFFERED

POSITIONS FILLED

Positions offered in neurology and number filled.

Percentage of neurology positions filled on Match Day.

NEUROLOGY

Neurology has greatly benefited from the recent explosion in technological research. In the past few years, the specialty has grown and changed direction; the focus is now shifting towards treatment, traditionally its weak area. At this time, it is still unclear how the field will be affected by the current changes brought about by managed care systems. It is predicted that primary care physicians will take increasing responsibility for such chronic problems as stroke, headaches, and uncomplicated seizures. However, more complex neurological problems will still require the care of a specialist. Currently, job opportunities for neurologists seeking private practices are readily available. In fact, some studies project a major shortage (up to 30%) in the supply of neurologists by the year 2010. For those pursuing an academic career, however, recent cut-backs in NIH funding could make fellowship and research positions increasingly difficult to obtain.

Neurology requires a 3-year residency program preceded by an internship year in medicine, surgery, or transitional medicine. It generally works to the resident's advantage to choose a medicine internship, which tends to be more relevant to later training in neurology. Depending on the program, the training might focus on one or two areas, such as anatomic neurology, diagnosis, or treatment techniques. Also, keep in mind that the patient population may influence the quality and focus of training in certain areas (eg, trauma-related neurologic diseases, HIV disease, or such chronic problems as stroke and epilepsy).

Match Numbers

Excellent training in neurology is readily available to nearly all interested applicants: only 1% of U.S. seniors went unmatched in the 1996 Match. The number of applications submitted to neurology programs has remained relatively stable in the past few years. The degree of competitiveness ranges widely, depending on the reputation of a given program. The neurology match at present is a "two-tier" match for PGY-2 positions in that PGY-2 positions that did not fill in the previous Match are offered alongside the PGY-2 positions scheduled to begin in a year and a half. In 1996, 369 of 476 positions offered for the first time were filled; 106 of 149 positions offered for the second time were also filled, resulting in an overall fill rate of 76% (Figures 3–6A, 3–6B).

Application Tips

Positions for neurology residencies are filled through an early match, which requires applicants to be diligent in completing their applications as soon as possible. Although deadlines for most programs are in November or December, all information should be submitted by October. Senior neurology rotation(s) should be completed in the summer of the fourth year to ensure early letters of recommendation. This is one field where the reputation of the letter-writer counts as much as the letter's substance. Generally, you should ask for a letter from the best known and most senior members of the neurology faculty, since their voices resonate loudest with the review committee. On another note, it could help to do away rotations at institutions of interest, although opinion is mixed on this issue.

To strengthen the application, include tangible proof of your commitment to the field of neurology, such as research experience, clinical volunteer experience, and publications. Some programs will also look at the location of your internship institution and the type of internship to which you applied. In general, many programs prefer a medical internship located at either the same institution or a similarly prestigious one.

Interview Tips

Interviews range from individual sessions lasting about 30–45 minutes to group sessions conducted by a panel of faculty members. Each program has a different style, so be sure to ask about their format when you call to schedule the appointment. Most of the time, the questions posed will gauge your dedication to the field. In addition to the common interview fare (see Chapter 9), some interviewers ask applicants to describe their research projects or offer their opinions on ethical issues in neurologic diagnosis and treatment.

For More Info . . .

▶ **Student information packet** available by calling or writing:

American Academy of Neurology
2221 University Ave, Southeast, #335
Minneapolis, MN 55414
(612) 623-2400

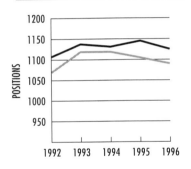

— POSITIONS OFFERED
— POSITIONS FILLED

Positions offered in obstetrics and gynecology and number filled.

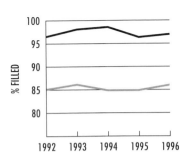

— TOTAL % FILLED
— U.S. % FILLED

Percentage of obstetrics and gynecology positions filled on Match Day.

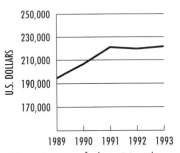

Mean income of obstetricians/gynecologists in U.S. dollars.

OBSTETRICS AND GYNECOLOGY

Obstetrics and gynecology has benefited from impressive biomedical advances in recent years. Improved maternal health care, *in vitro* fertilization, and better high-risk pregnancy management have expanded the practice of OB/GYN, allowing for better patient care. On the downside, the threat of litigation and the accompanying high professional liability insurance premiums continue to be key, thorny issues. Recent upgrading in the training of midwives and nurse practitioners to perform obstetrical duties further increases the competition for work within the field, prompting many OB/GYN practitioners to concentrate on gynecology.

In spite of the obstacles, demand to enter the field remains relatively strong. Medical students are attracted to the specialty because of the opportunity to work with a wide age range of women patients, the opportunity to provide long-term patient care, and the ability to combine basic medical care with surgical procedures. Also, the mean income in obstetrics and gynecology has remained steady through 1993 (Figure 3–7C).

Residencies in obstetrics and gynecology involve 4 years of training, followed by 2 years of post-graduate practice to become board-eligible. Patient care, including prenatal care, delivery techniques, routine gynecologic care, and gynecologic oncology care, make up the bulk of training. OB/GYN residents are eligible for certificates of specialty following 2- to 3-year post-residency fellowships in maternal-fetal medicine, gynecologic oncology, and reproductive endocrinology. On another note, keep in mind that programs at hospitals with religious affiliations may offer little or no experience in many aspects of infertility management, *in vitro* fertilization, and therapeutic and elective abortions.

Match Numbers

Competition for training positions remains rigorous, especially on the West Coast. The falling number of deliveries and surgeries performed in teaching hospitals means that more programs in this specialty are cutting spots. In 1996, 1090 of 1125 available residency spots were filled through the NRMP, resulting in a high fill rate of 97%. OB/GYN consistently carries a high non-match rate in the Match (Figures 3–7A, 3–7B). In 1995, 12% of U.S. seniors who ranked only OB/GYN programs failed to match.

Application Tips

It is important for interested applicants to complete a senior rotation in OB/GYN and to collect strong letters of support from well-known faculty members in this field. Some prestigious programs have suggested that students try to complete away rotations at institutions that interest them in order to increase their chances of being granted an interview. USMLE Step 1 scores, AΩA status, and the number of honors received are criteria used by many programs. Good evaluations in surgical rotations will also increase the applicant's strength. All application material should be submitted as early as possible, usually by October. The recommended number of applications depends on the strength of the applicant, but a general range of 15 to 20 is a fair norm.

For the 1996 Match, the AAMC introduced the Electronic Residency Application Service (ERAS) (see pg. 83) to OB/GYN as a replacement for the traditional "snail-mail" method of application. Students who used ERAS generally give it high marks. Stay in touch with your OB/GYN department and your dean's office for details.

Interview Tips

OB/GYN interviews are usually conducted in December and January. When you call to schedule, be aware that many programs have only a limited time period, during which they interview large groups of applicants. The earlier you submit your application, the more choices of dates you'll have. Interview schedules run long, lasting from 8 AM to 5 PM, with 3 to 4 interviews of 30 to 45 minutes each. These might be individual or group interviews, depending on the program. Be ready to present a case or to discuss some technical/ethical issues in the specialty. If you've done research, know your work inside-out, for you will be questioned on it. For the most part, interviews are cordial and informal, offering the interviewer an opportunity to assess your personality.

For More Info . . .

▶ **Student information packet** available by calling or writing:

American College of Obstetricians and Gynecologists
409 12th Street, SW
Washington, DC 20024
(202) 638-5577

OPHTHALMOLOGY

Thanks in large part to innovations in surgical and laser techniques, ophthalmology has recently taken off as a high-tech surgical and medical specialty. Unfortunately, the opportunity for employment has not kept up. As is often the case in non-primary care specialties, work in ophthalmology in large- and medium-sized cities is difficult to find, though not impossible. Because of the popularity of the training field, newly graduated ophthalmologists face sharpening competition with one another for the same patient pool, especially in larger cities. The cost-cutting policies that accompany managed care have shifted many procedures, such as routine vision check, refractions, and general eye care, toward the less costly optometrists. Furthermore, Medicare has been lowering reimbursements for cataract surgery. More patients with such chronic conditions as diabetes, glaucoma, and multiple sclerosis are being managed non-surgically by teams of optometrists and primary MDs. Some ophthalmologists are discovering that they have to market themselves to offer more than just surgical management of diseases in order to maintain a steady patient population.

Residencies in ophthalmology require a year of internship, followed by 3 years of specialty training. The residents often rotate through both surgical and non-surgical rotations, learning surgical techniques as well as medical diagnosis and management of eye diseases. Board eligibility is achieved immediately after finishing residency. Currently, there is no certification for subspecialties. However, residents can tailor their training to reflect areas of interest, such as cataract, glaucoma, or retinal surgery.

Match Numbers

Although ophthalmology remains a competitive specialty, it is no longer considered untouchable by the non-stellar applicant. In the past several years, there has been a steady decline in the number of applicants. As a result, the nonmatch rate for U.S. seniors has dropped from 45% in the mid-1980s to 6% in 1996. In comparison, the non-match rate was 13% for emergency medicine applicants and 38% for ENT applicants in 1996. On the other hand, international medical graduates continue to fare badly, with a non-match rate of 66%. In 1996, 441 of 454 available positions in ophthalmology were filled, 97% fill rate (Figures 3–8A, 3–8B, 3–8C).

Application Tips

Positions in ophthalmology residencies are offered primarily through the Ophthalmology Matching Program conducted by August Colenbrander, MD. Given the competition to enter the field, the potential applicant should concentrate on doing well on the USMLE Step 1, in core senior electives, as well as the senior ophthalmology rotation. Supportive evaluations and recommendations from the senior ophthalmology faculty will clinch a strong application. Since this is another small field in which most department heads know one another, connections can play an important part in getting you that interview. Any research experience, especially work resulting in publications and/or presentations, should be included in your CV and will be viewed favorably. Most programs accept a universal application that must be submitted to a Central Application Service by mid-October. At present, most applicants are advised to submit about 20 to 35 applications.

UNDERSTAND THE DIFFERENCES BETWEEN OPHTHALMOLOGY AND OPTOMETRY, AND THEIR POLITICAL TURF BATTLES.

OPHTHALMOLOGY IS NOT AS COMPETITIVE AS IT USED TO BE.

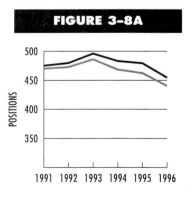

FIGURE 3-8A

POSITIONS

500
450
400
350

1991 1992 1993 1994 1995 1996

— POSITIONS OFFERED
— POSITIONS FILLED

Positions offered in ophthalmology and number filled.

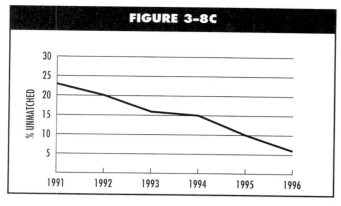

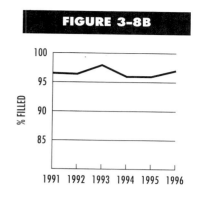

Percentage of U.S. seniors unmatched in ophthalmology on Match Day.

Percentage of ophthalmology positions filled on Match Day.

Many advisers also suggest that you apply to a mix of strong and weak programs in order to increase your probability of matching.

Interview Tips

Similar to those of other surgical subspecialties, interviews for ophthalmology verge on the formal. Often, the applicants will meet with the department head, one or two senior faculty members, and at least one resident. Most interviews last from 30 to 45 minutes, with many of the questions geared toward assessing the applicant's interest in the field, clinical and research background, and personality. There could be some clinical questions asked, depending on the interviewer. Generally, take these interviews seriously, be professional and enthusiastic, but don't stress out. Interviewers do not ordinarily grill applicants. However, given the competitiveness of the field, interviewers sometimes ask about your contingency plans in case you don't match in ophthalmology.

For More Info . . .

▶ *Envision Ophthalmology: A Practical Guide to Ophthalmology as a Career Choice.* A free publication of the American Academy of Ophthalmology, it includes general information about the application process, as well as a practical discussion of factors to consider in selecting and assessing an ophthalmology program. To receive this excellent career guide, call or write:

American Academy of Ophthalmology
P.O. Box 7424
San Francisco, CA 94120-7424
(415) 561-8500

ORTHOPEDICS

Orthopedic surgery continues to be a rewarding field. These specialists have opportunities to combine surgical techniques and orthopedic hardware (eg, microsurgery and joint prostheses) with work in physical rehabilitation for the treatment of acute and chronic orthopedic problems. Earnings for orthopedic surgeons continue to be well above average. However, increasing professional liability insurance premiums and overhead costs are reducing overall compensation.

Residencies require at least 5 years of training, with up to 2 years spent in general surgery or other approved medical or surgical residencies and the last 3 years in an orthopedic surgery program. A post-residency practice period is required before you become board-eligible. Subspecialty training is available in hand surgery, spinal surgery, sports medicine, orthopedic trauma, and pediatric orthopedics.

Match Numbers

In 1996, 99% of the 504 available spots were filled through the Match, ranking orthopedic surgery among the most competitive surgical specialties. Predictably, it consistently has one of the highest non-match rates in the NRMP Match. In 1995, nearly 16% of U.S. seniors who ranked only orthopedic programs did not match (Figures 3–9A, 3–9B, 3–9C).

Application Tips

Orthopedic surgery is becoming more academic. Thus, research experience is virtually a requirement for an application to be seriously considered by a prestigious program. Strong evaluations in the orthopedic surgery rotation, enthusiastic recommendations from the faculty members in the field, and high board scores are key ingredients of a strong application. It is common for residency programs to use USMLE Step 1 scores to screen applicants, with a cutoff ranging from the 75th to the 85th percentile. Some residency programs encourage students to take an audition elective at their institution in order to be considered for interviews. However, be aware that you will have to turn in a stellar performance on these away rotations. It would also help to select a mentor who has seniority in the department. Given the "good old boy" network at some institutions, establishing connections may open a few more doors. Deadlines for applications range from October to late December; however, be sure to send in all your application materials by early October, because interview spots fill quickly.

Interview Tips

Interviews in orthopedic surgery are extremely difficult to obtain, so if you are offered one, it means that you've proven yourself academically. During the interviews, be prepared for anything. You could be asked questions probing personality type or to discuss a range of political, ethical, and sometimes, humorous subjects. Female applicants may encounter off-color remarks or inappropriate questions in a specialty that still sports a "jock" image. If you've done research, know your stuff so that you can answer questions quickly and clearly. Interviewers mainly look for something distinctive about the person and try to determine whether he or she will fit in with the rest of the residents in the program. Interviews are mostly conducted on an individual basis, with three to four sessions of about 30 to 45 minutes each.

ONE IN SIX U.S. SENIORS WENT UNMATCHED IN ORTHOPEDIC SURGERY.

HIGH BOARD SCORES, AΩA, MANY HONORS, AND RESEARCH ARE THE KEYS TO SUCCESS.

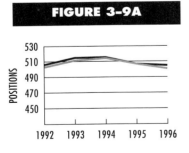

FIGURE 3-9A

— POSITIONS OFFERED
— POSITIONS FILLED

Positions offered in orthopedic surgery and number filled.

For More Info . . .

▶ For a brochure on careers in orthopedic surgery, call or write:
American Academy of Orthopedic Surgeons
6300 North River Road
Rosemont, IL 60018-4262
(708) 823-7186

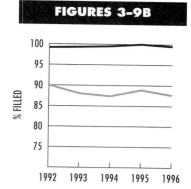

FIGURES 3-9B

—— TOTAL % FILLED
—— U.S. % FILLED

Percentage of orthopedic surgery positions filled on Match Day.

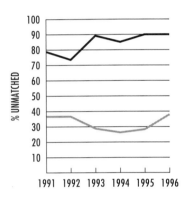

— POSITIONS OFFERED
— POSITIONS FILLED

Positions offered in otolaryngology and number filled.

— IMGS
— U.S. SENIORS

Percentage of U.S. seniors unmatched in otolaryngology on Match Day.

"ENT" IS A FOUR LETTER WORD TO MANY OTOLARYNGOLOGISTS.

OTOLARYNGOLOGY

Ear, nose, and throat (ENT) physicians will continue to be a small subspecialty in demand. Although the primary care specialties will likely take over allergy treatment and immunology as well as simple procedures like tympanotomy, ENT physicians will continue to have roles in academics, ENT oncology, and the growing fields of facial plastics and otologic implants. Most ENT programs are 5 years and include 1 or 2 years of preliminary surgery. A few of the more prestigious, heavily academic programs add another year for research. Many ENT graduates pursue fellowship training in one of a number of subspecialty fields, including head and neck surgery, laryngology, otology, neurotology, rhinology, and plastic and reconstructive surgery.

Match Numbers

Otolaryngology continues to be an extremely competitive specialty. Both supply and demand have been steady: last year there were 430 applicants for approximately 240 positions. Only one position of 240 offered initially went unfilled in the 1996 Match (Figure 3–10A). Thirty-eight percent of U.S. seniors went unmatched; foreign medical graduates fared much worse, with a dismal 90% nonmatch rate (Figure 3–10B).

Application Tips

Strong applicants in this specialty have impressive all-around credentials, including research experience. USMLE Step 1 scores are often used by program directors as a screening tool, with some ENT applicants reporting cutoffs between the 75th and 85th percentiles. A recent study found a strong correlation between high medical school GPAs (if available), high board scores, high class rank (if available), honors in both junior surgery and medicine, and AΩA selection and ENT matching success. Some of the very competitive ENT programs suggest doing an audition rotation at their hospital to increase your likelihood of being invited for an interview. Otherwise, it's a good idea to do externships if you are aiming for specific programs where your application is less competitive than you'd like.

The average number of applications per student has risen dramatically over the past decade, from 12 in 1985 to an average of 33 in 1995. Unfortunately, the number of available positions and the number of interviews offered have largely remained unchanged.

Because there are only about 100 programs in ENT and only a few spots per program, you are operating at a serious disadvantage if you have to apply in a particular geographic region. Virtually all ENT applicants complete the 9-page universal ENT application, which must be received by a Central Application Service by mid-September. On the last page of this form, there is room to attach the names and addresses of the programs to which you want the application forwarded. The more programs you apply to, the higher the cost. Be sure to emphasize any research experience in your application. You are allowed to submit no more than three letters of recommendation. The most balanced approach is to submit two letters from ENT faculty and one from a clinical attending from another major clerkship (eg, medicine, OB/GYN, etc). The easiest advice to follow? **Never** use the colloquial term "ENT" in your application or interview visit; always say "otolaryngology."

Interview Tips

Most ENT interviews are scheduled in November and December. If you're offered an interview at one program, it would not hurt to call other programs nearby where you have applied and ask if they are willing to grant you an interview while you are in the area. Most ENT programs, however, have only two to three interview dates per season. As a result, clustering interviews is often very difficult. Be ready to criss-cross the country to get all the interviews you need.

An applicant will typically sit for four to six interviews during the visit, each lasting 15 to 30 minutes. This schedule usually includes an interview with the department chairperson. Emphasize the strengths and interests you can offer that are most compatible with the philosophy of the particular program. It is always a good idea to highlight your academic and research interests when you are interviewed by the department chair, even if the program is more clinically oriented. Moreover, feel free to drop names, assuming that the interview is going well and that you are well liked by the people whose names you drop. ENT is a small field where anyone who's anyone knows everyone.

Note that if you are a competitive candidate, programs may try to ask you how you are ranking them. If that program is **not** your top choice, then tell the interviewer(s) that you regard their program highly but cannot in fairness make that decision until you have finished your interviews. If the program turns out to be one of your top choices, feel free to mention that fact in your follow-up thank-you letter.

For More Info . . .

American Academy of Otolaryngology—
    Head and Neck Surgery
1 Prince Street
Alexandria, VA 22314
(703) 836-4444

PATHOLOGY

Over the past 4 years, the total number of pathology residencies available, as well as the percentage of positions filled on Match Day, have increased. More applicants have come to recognize that this specialty offers both work flexibility and technical challenges. Because of the rise in surgical and needle biopsies as part of the diagnostic process, pathologists are becoming more active in direct patient care. The downside of the specialty, however, continues to be an increase in the number of government and laboratory regulations, which result in more paperwork, less time for actual patient care, decreased funding for research programs, and curtailed patient contact compared with other fields. Although the amount of work has remained the same or increased over the past few years, pathologists' incomes have remained steady or decreased (Figure 3–11C). Specialists currently in the work force find that they have to work longer hours for the same pay. Furthermore, private practices are not hiring as many pathologists, especially in large urban centers. As a result, more residents are delaying graduation from the training programs and choosing instead to take 1 or 2 extra years to acquire more distinctive fellowship skills to make themselves desirable to potential employers. Many are also choosing research as an alternative to hospital practice. It is still unclear at this time if the trend of decreasing job opportunities in pathology will continue in the future.

To be board-qualified in either anatomic or clinical pathology requires a minimum of 4 years. Entering students should look at combined programs, which offer a 5-year residency covering both types of pathology giving you a sort of bilingual appeal. Certified in one specialty, you might be limited to working in large hospitals that can afford to employ separate specialists.

Pathology training is relatively flexible, as long as the resident completes the core rotations required for board certifications, such as surgical pathology, cytopathology, autopsy, and subspecialty rotations particular to each emphasis. He or she is then free to take elective courses, conduct research, or acquire further training in a specialized area of interest, such as forensic pathology.

Match Numbers

In spite of improved recognition, the field of pathology still suffers from a shortage of qualified applicants. In 1996, only 331 of 426 positions offered, or 78%, were filled through the NRMP Match (Figures 3–11A, 3–11B). Given the possible decline in job prospects, pathology programs will continue to cut the number of positions offered.

Application Tips

Because training programs in pathology have different emphases, it is important to find one that matches your career goals. This is especially true for combined clinical and anatomic pathology programs, which may be strong in only one department. After you select your emphasis, the next step is to demonstrate your desire to enter the field of pathology to the programs of your choice. A strong evaluation in the senior elective, accompanied by solid letters of recommendation (at least one from a pathologist), is essential in this process. Most programs use their own application forms instead of the Universal Application supplied by the NRMP, so be sure to request the ap-

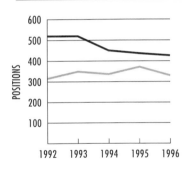

POSITIONS OFFERED

POSITIONS FILLED

Positions offered in pathology and number filled.

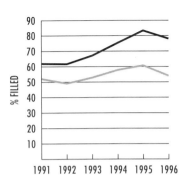

TOTAL % FILLED

U.S. % FILLED

Percentage of pathology positions filled on Match Day.

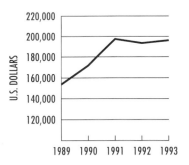

Mean income of pathologists in U.S. dollars.

propriate information and forms early. Application material should be completed as soon as possible, preferably by mid-November.

Interview Tips

Given the less than glamorous image of pathology, most interviewers will be extremely curious to know why you are interested in the field. Be prepared to answer many questions about your particular interests, any research background, or any plans for your future career. Interviews often last about 30 minutes, with three to six interviews a day, depending on whether you are applying to the combined or single program. In general, pathology interviews are relaxed, with only occasional tough questions. Expect to answer some questions about your post-residency plans, such as research, extra training, or going straight into private practice.

If you are ranked highly by a pathology program, you can expect some pressure to rank the program highly in return. Contrary to the official Match guidelines, many program directors will contact strong applicants and question them about their rankings. Be sure to keep your cool and not be pressured into making a "commitment" prematurely.

For More Info . . .

▶ *Student Information Packet.* This free packet includes several articles and a slick brochure about career opportunities in pathology. The College of American Pathologists also produces a promotional video that it lends out at no cost. To receive an information packet or borrow the video, call or write:

> College of American Pathologists
> 325 Waukegan Road
> North Field, IL 60093
> (800) 323-4040

▶ American Society of Clinical Pathologists
> 2100 West Harrison Street
> Chicago, IL 60612-3798
> (312) 738-1336

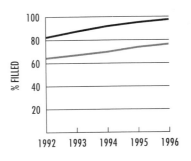

Positions offered in pediatrics and number filled.

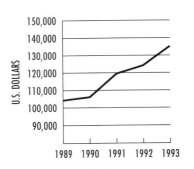

Percentage of pediatrics positions filled on Match Day.

Mean income of pediatricians in U.S. dollars.

PEDIATRICS

Pediatrics has a reputation as an easygoing specialty. Satisfied pediatricians enjoy developing relationships with their young patients as they grow up. Unlike family physicians, pediatricians can evaluate the whole family without being responsible for every member's medical care. Today the field is seeing more routine procedures and well-child care done by nurse practitioners, physician assistants, and family practitioners, which means pediatricians can focus on the care of the seriously ill. The trend in residency training favors increased ambulatory care. The current health care climate assures excellent employment prospects for pediatricians. In addition, preventive health care, an integral part of pediatrics, will be encouraged and better compensated (Figure 3–12D). However, the long arm of managed care is threatening to squeeze pediatric subspecialists and the population of children's hospitals, which have high operating expenses because of the nature of their training mission.

Pediatric programs can be roughly classified by setting: children's versus non-children's hospital. Children's hospitals have more pediatrics specialists available and in general offer more comprehensive training and education. In a children's hospital, everything is geared toward kids, from the intubating equipment in the ER to the wallpaper in the CT units. Children's hospitals tend to be located in large cities and have more of a tertiary care focus. Good children's hospitals have affiliations with adult centers for delivery room experience.

By contrast, residencies in non-children's hospitals provide more interaction with faculty and house staff from other primary care specialties that involve children, such as family practice, OB/GYN and internal medicine. These programs can be further categorized into community, university, and county/municipal settings. These are discussed in more detail in Chapter 4.

Match Numbers

Along with internal medicine and family practice, pediatrics has surged in popularity among medical students. In the 1996 Match, 97.5% of the 2017 available pediatric positions were filled, leaving only 51 positions available for the Scramble. In contrast, over 400 positions went unfilled in the 1991 Match (Figures 3–12A, 3–12B, 3–12C). Many expect pediatric residency applications to continue to increase over the next few years.

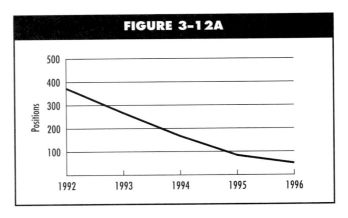

Number of unfilled positions in pediatrics.

Application Tips

Though pediatrics is on the upswing, securing an interview is still mostly a matter of scheduling, since most programs do not seriously screen applicants. In fact, many programs ask the applicant to call in automatically after submitting the application to schedule an interview. Therefore, we strongly advise that you submit your applications when programs first accept them in the early fall. Do not be one of the many qualified applicants who get locked out of interviews each year because of poor timing. Though the number of applications you should submit depends on your strength as a candidate and the programs to which you are applying, most applicants are generally advised to submit 8 to 12 applications.

It goes without saying that your personal statement and CV should emphasize any involvement with children, community or public health care, or volunteer activity. As in the other primary care specialties, the type of individual you are and your long-term goals will provide fodder for question-and-answer sessions.

Interview Tips

Most interviews for pediatrics programs are scheduled from late November through January. The interview day typically runs from 8 AM to 3 PM. Expect two to four interview sessions, 20 to 45 minutes in length. Interviews in this specialty are generally low-key and non-confrontational. In addition to having the qualities typically desired in all house officers, you must package yourself as an individual who interacts well with parents and children. Good interpersonal skills are a must. Remember that most of your interviewers are parents themselves.

For More Info . . .

▶ *Pediatrics Information Packet.* In addition to a general profile of the specialty, this packet includes fact sheets detailing current socioeconomic statistics on pediatric practice. To receive this information, gratis, call or write:

> American Academy of Pediatrics
> 141 Northwest Point Blvd
> Elk Grove Village, IL 60007
> (800) 433-9016, ext. 7914 or
> (708) 228-5005, ext. 7914

▶ *Selecting a Pediatric Residency: An Employment Guide.* This is a comprehensive, step-by-step guide to selecting, applying to, and interviewing at pediatric residency programs. It also discusses family and marriage considerations, such employment issues as contract and salary guidelines, and certification licensing requirements. It's available to medical students for $5 plus shipping costs. To order, call or write:

> AAP, Publications Department
> PO Box 927
> Elk Grove Village, IL 60009-0927
> (800) 433-9016

MOST APPLICANTS WHO DID NOT GET INTERVIEWS SIMPLY APPLIED TOO LATE.

► Kappy, M: The pediatric residency program of the future: I. The changing face of today's private pediatric practice. *Am J Dis Child* 1987;141:945. Though somewhat dated, this series of articles addresses many issues that remain current in pediatrics.

► Kappy, M: The pediatric residency program of the future: II. Tomorrow's private pediatric practice: A change in roles. *Am J Dis Child* 1987;141:1045.

► Kappy, M: The pediatric residency program of the future: III. Modifying pediatric residency training programs. *Am J Dis Child* 1987;141:1156.

PSYCHIATRY

The widespread shift toward primary care has affected psychiatry in several ways. Issues often mentioned include lack of adequate provision for mental health care by most insurance plans or HMOs. The shift of psychotherapeutic care to primary care physicians, psychologists, and social workers also cuts into the available work for board-certified psychiatrists. Although practitioners report a high satisfaction rate with the work involved—and the mean income in this field has been relatively steady (Figure 3–13C)—many also register anxiety about the future of the specialty.

Residencies in psychiatry generally require 1 year of internship, preferably in preliminary medicine, followed by 3 years of training in psychiatry. Some have a fourth year with emphasis in neurology or geriatrics. Depending on the program, training can emphasize either psychotherapy or the biological aspects of mental illness. Thus, it is important to determine whether the orientation of a particular program matches your expectations and field of interest.

Match Numbers

Since 1991, the number of positions offered in the field of psychiatry has been decreasing. Though applications in psychiatry have surged in the past two years, the specialty remains relatively easy to enter. In 1995, 771 of 917 available spots, or 84% (up from 68%, in 1994), were filled through the Match (Figures 3–13A, 3–13B).

Application Tips

Unlike other fields, personal statements for psychiatry are traditionally substantial in length (two-page personal statements are OK) and should discuss in some detail your interest in and understanding of the field. Except for a few prestigious programs, most do not pay much attention to board scores. Rather, emphasis is placed on the applicant's clinical evaluations, especially in psychiatry rotations. Good letters of recommendation, as well as documented interests in the field, such as prior research or involvement in mental health care, will further strengthen your application. Again, early completion of application material is important. The average number of applications submitted ranges from 10 to 15, with about 8 to 10 interviews recommended.

Interview Tips

During the interview day, the applicant has an average of 4 interviews, lasting 45 to 60 minutes each. Questions tend to probe the applicant's desire to enter psychiatry and his or her ability to interact with other people. It's a good idea to review strengths and weaknesses ahead of time, since many of the questions may deal with your personality. Some applicants compare these interviews to psychoanalytical sessions placing you on the proverbial couch. Little or no pimping is involved, except regarding the candidate's previous research experience. In general, expect to meet psychiatrists who seek potential colleagues with stable personalities and good interpersonal skills. According to experienced applicants, an unspoken purpose of the interview is to rule out obvious psychopathology.

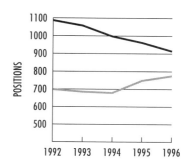

— POSITIONS OFFERED
— POSITIONS FILLED

Positions offered in psychiatry and number filled.

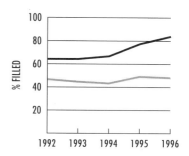

— TOTAL % FILLED
— U.S. % FILLED

Percentage of psychiatry positions filled on Match Day.

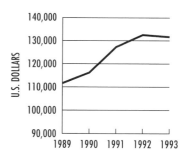

Mean income of psychiatrists in U.S. dollars.

ONE PURPOSE OF THE INTERVIEW IS TO RULE OUT OBVIOUS PSYCHOPATHOLOGY.

For More Info . . .

▶ *Directory of Psychiatric Residency Training Programs.* Although this directory is not updated as often as AMA-FREIDA, it has a more logical, user-friendly format. Information unique to the directory includes contact name and number for student electives, house staff contact names, and diagrams of a typical resident rotation schedule. The directory also offers general advice about residency applications. It's available at your psychiatry department or can be ordered for $25 with a student discount from:

American Psychiatric Press, Inc.
1400 K Street NW
Washington, DC 20005
(800) 368-5777

RADIOLOGY

Radiology is a field that has grown tremendously in the last decade, thanks primarily to technological advances in imaging techniques. Radiologists continue to enjoy a good lifestyle, relatively high income (Figure 3–14C), and flexible work hours. The advent of managed care, however, and the focus on primary care pose worrisome trends for the field. Practitioners in other fields, such as cardiology, gastroenterology, and urology, are performing many imaging guided procedures. Employment, especially in large cities with a high density of MDs, is increasingly difficult to find. Many hospitals are hiring fewer radiologists, thus making the ones already employed work longer hours. Cutbacks in trained technologists and ancillary personnel in the radiology department also cause increased workloads and heavier paperwork.

Training in radiology generally requires 1 year of internship followed by 4 years of diagnostic radiology. The internship year can be satisfied by completion of a transitional, surgical, or preliminary medicine year. The style of radiology training depends on the institution, but all institutions will cover the major imaging modalities, including nuclear medicine. Post-residency fellowships (1–2 years) are offered in a wide variety of organ-based specialties, including neuroimaging, vascular/interventional, mammography/women's imaging, body imaging, chest, and musculoskeletal; and in modality-based fellowships, such as computed tomography, magnetic resonance, ultrasonography, and nuclear medicine.

Match Numbers

Traditionally a competitive specialty, radiology proved much easier to enter in 1996. This change resulted primarily from an increase in the number of available training positions. In 1996, 703 of the 1154 available PGY-1 and PGY-2 positions were filled through the NRMP on Match Day, resulting in a 61% fill rate—down from 89.8% in 1994 (Figures 3–14A, 3–14B). Only 1.5% of U.S. seniors applying in radiology in 1996 went unmatched.

Application Tips

Strong evaluations in the senior clinical rotations, especially radiology, support the successful application. High board scores and excellent letters of recommendation by senior radiology faculty members are next in importance. Research experience or a technical background prior to entering medical school is viewed favorably. As with other competitive specialties, early completion of application material is important. You will need to be well-organized to coordinate applications for both internship and residency positions. Although the competitiveness of the applicants may be declining, applicants are usually advised to submit 15 to 20 in order to obtain a comfortable 8 to 12 interviews.

Interview Tips

Because of the small number of spots available, residency programs in radiology tend to offer interviews only to strong applicants in whom they are seriously interested. Each candidate's visit typically includes two to five interviews, 15 to 30 minutes in length. Interviews for radiology often tend to be relaxed, placing the major emphasis on the applicant's reason for entering the field and interviewing at this particular institution (Table 3–2). You

UNDERSTAND THE DIFFERENCES BETWEEN DIAGNOSTIC RADIOLOGY, NUCLEAR MEDICINE, AND RADIATION ONCOLOGY.

FIGURES 3–14A–B

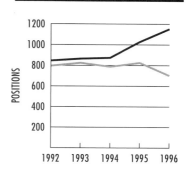

— POSITIONS OFFERED
— POSITIONS FILLED

Positions offered in radiology and number filled.

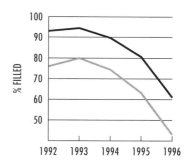

— TOTAL % FILLED
— U.S. % FILLED

Percentage of radiology positions filled on Match Day.

FIGURE 3-14C

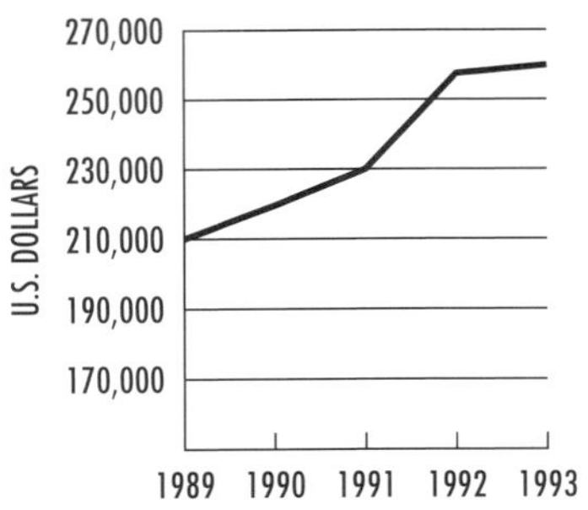

Mean income of radiologists in U.S. dollars.

TABLE 3–2. Most commonly asked interview questions in Radiology.

Interview Question	% of Applicants Who Received Question
Why are you going into radiology?	71%
Why did you apply here or why do you want to come here?	32%
What do you see yourself doing in the future?	23%
Are you applying to other programs? If so, what are they?	23%
Why should we choose you?	16%
What do you do in your spare time?	13%
Name your strengths and weaknesses.	13%
Do you have any questions?	13%
How did you become interested in radiology?	10%

might be invited to attend a clinical case conference, but almost no one expects you to be able to read an x-ray on the spot. Quantifying a "good eye" in radiology is even harder than evaluating manual dexterity for a surgical field, so programs don't even try.

The interviewers will also attempt to predict how well you can relate to other professionals, since much of radiology consists of consulting work (ie, being a "doctor's doctor"). In general, these sessions are low-stress, with little or no pimping involved. Let the program showcase its strengths; don't ask questions that highlight its weaknesses. For example, if they don't have a $5 million high-field research magnet, don't ask about the (im)possibility of their buying one for you. On the other hand, if they have one, feel free to discuss its relevance to your research.

For More Info . . .

▶ *Career Information Packet.* This packet includes a brochure describing the field of radiology as well as several articles describing the job prospects, average earnings, and practice characteristics. This information can be obtained free of charge by calling or writing:

American College of Radiology
1891 Preston White Drive
Reston, VA 22091
(800) ACR-LINE

SURGERY

General surgery residencies have increased in popularity over the past few years, thus making the field increasingly competitive for aspiring surgeons. The specialty boasts a number of benefits: the chance to apply technical and procedural skills toward quick resolutions of medical problems, good doctor/patient relationships, and relatively high income (Figure 3–15C). Drawbacks include long hours, rigorous training, increasing paperwork, and the intrusion of such prickly non-clinical issues as malpractice liability, government regulations, and third-party payers. Generally, most surgeons remain highly satisfied with their work, notwithstanding the changes they make in their practices to accommodate HMOs and other complications.

Surgical residencies require a minimum of 5 years of training, with some programs requiring as many as 3 additional research years. These often come in the middle or later portion of the residency, at a time when residents can also moonlight. Subspecialty training includes critical care surgery, hand surgery, pediatric surgery, plastic surgery, vascular surgery, and trauma surgery.

Match Numbers

Surgery remains very competitive. In 1996, 1003 positions of the 1004 available were filled through the NRMP on Match Day, resulting in a 99.9% fill rate (Figures 3–15A, 3–15B). The general surgery match has consistently high non-match rates. In 1996, 1 of 5 U.S. seniors who ranked only surgery programs did not match.

Application Tips

Before applying, you should think about whether you would be happier in a clinical or a research-oriented program, noting that length of training varies from one type of program to the other. Generally, strong evaluations in the senior surgical rotations are essential to successful applications. The *pièce de résistance* would be a strong letter from the chief of surgery. Programs with an academic slant will definitely consider the applicant's research background fundamental to the evaluation process, whereas those with a clinical focus will attempt to determine the applicant's potential to be a good surgeon. For advice and connection purposes, it's always helpful to find a mentor who is well known in the field. As with other competitive residencies, early completion of application material is important. Although the desired number of applications depends on the applicant's quality, the average ranges from 15 to 20, with a goal of at least 10 to 12 interviews suggested.

Interview Tips

As one applicant put it, the interview is used mainly to eliminate malignant personalities. They may be tolerated at the attending level, but no one wants to deal with this problem in a junior resident. Interview committees often have a good idea of how they are going to rank you before they even meet you. Interview days are usually Saturdays and often consist of 2 to 3 sessions, lasting 30 to 45 minutes each. Occasionally, one is asked to present a clinical case or to discuss how to deal with the stress of a surgical residency. Often, interviews are laid-back, with little or no pimping. However, academic programs tend to opt for more pointed questions, inquiring about your research background and any current projects. Try to learn something about the program's reputation for research.

FIGURES 3-15A-C

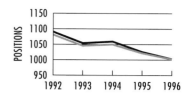

Positions offered in surgery and number filled.

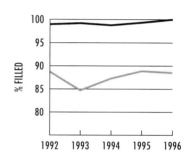

Percentage of surgery positions filled on Match Day.

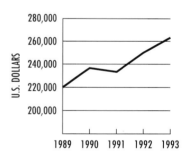

Mean income of surgeons in U.S. dollars.

For More Info . . .

► Johansen K, Heimbach DM: *So You Want to Be a Surgeon . . . A Medical Student Guide to Finding and Matching With the Best Possible Residency*. This book includes a brief but very helpful discussion of surgical residency applications. The greater part of the book is devoted to descriptions of most of the surgery programs in the United States and Puerto Rico. The authors attempt to classify programs by the caliber of the house staff. The book is in some medical bookstores, and can also be ordered for about $12 from:

> Educational Clearinghouse
> Department of Surgery
> Southern Illinois University
>   School of Medicine
> PO Box 19230
> Springfield, IL 62794
> (217) 785-3835

► *The Surgical Career Handbook*. This glossy booklet provides an overview of surgery and profiles its subspecialties. The information, however, is often too general to be useful. This publication is available for $7 from:

> American College of Surgeons
> 55 East Erie Street
> Chicago, IL 60611
> (312) 664-4050

TRANSITIONAL YEAR PROGRAM (TYP)

For those on a quest for a flexible internship, TYPs continue to be a popular choice. In contrast to the preliminary medicine or preliminary surgery years, transitional internships allow for exposure to many other fields, such as OB/GYN, ER, orthopedics, pediatrics, anesthesia, as well as traditional medicine and surgery. Transitional internships consist of multiple rotations through different departments. The length of each rotation, and the type of work involved are usually extremely flexible and can be tailored to fit each individual's need. Some programs, however, will have certain required core rotations that must be satisfied. In general, the requirements are minimal and can be easily fulfilled.

The variety of experience is ideal for anyone entering a residency, such as emergency medicine, in which a wide base of knowledge is desirable.

Other students take a TYP because they're undecided on a specialty but this can prove a difficult undertaking. By the time your year starts, the application process is already upon you. In addition, finding time for interviews during the year can be impossible. Make sure you reach an understanding with the program director/chief resident regarding time you will need to apply and interview. If you can't take sufficient time off, you may be better off taking a year off for research or an MPH.

Match Numbers

TYPs are not very competitive. In 1996, 811 positions of 1072 available spots were filled, giving a fill rate of 75.7% (Figures 3–16A, 3–16B).

Application Tips

As with most internship programs, the competitiveness of the program depends on the reputation of the institution and the flexibility of the program. Applicants should have strong clinical evaluations, strong letters of recommendation, and convincing reasons for seeking a transitional internship. Board scores tend to be less important, except at very prestigious institutions. Early submission of application material is important. The recommended deadline is early November, despite the February date posted by many programs.

Interview Tips

Interviews are casually conducted and are even optional for some programs. Usually, the applicant will be scheduled for 2 or 3 sessions, lasting 30 minutes each. Questions try to appraise the candidate's ability to fit in with the program, his or her desire for a transitional residency, and post-internship plans. Some transitional medicine residency directors do not like having their program used as "down time" for consideration of career plans, so be prepared to discuss your long-term career goals.

UNDECIDED STUDENTS ARE SOMETIMES BETTER SERVED BY TAKING A YEAR OFF FOR RESEARCH OR AN MPH.

FIGURES 3-16A-B

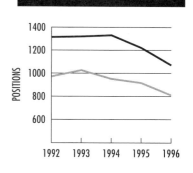

— POSITIONS OFFERED
— POSITIONS FILLED

Positions offered in TYPs and number filled.

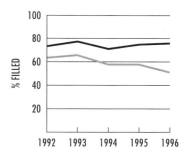

— TOTAL % FILLED
— U.S. % FILLED

Percentage of TYP positions filled on Match Day.

For More Info . . .

► *Transitional Year Program Directory*. More popularly known as the "Purple Book." This annually updated directory is available at your student affairs office. You can order your own copy by calling or writing:

> Association for Hospital Medical Education
> Council of Transitional Year Program Directors
> 1200 19th Street NW, Suite 300
> Washington, DC 20035-2401
> (202) 857-1196

► Kimball Mohn, MD
Chair of the Council of Transitional Year Program Directors
Mercy Hospital, Department of Medicine
1400 Locust Street
Pittsburgh, PA 15219
(412) 232-8080

REFERENCES

Baker JD et al: Selection of anesthesiology residents. *Acad Med* 1994;68:161.

Calhoun K et al: The resident selection process in otolaryngology-head and neck surgery. *Arch Otolaryngol Head Neck Surg* 1990;116:1041.

Center for Health Policy Research, *Physician Marketplace Statistics 1994*. Chicago: American Medical Association, 1994.

Center for Health Policy Research, *Socioeconomic Characteristics of Medical Practice 1995*. Chicago: American Medical Association, 1995.

Ende J: The 1995 match: Internal medicine and other generalist specialties attract more US grads. *APDIM Newsletter*, March 1995.

Featherstone H, Ramsey P: Analysis of selection criteria for medical residents. *Am J Med* 1983;75.

Kahn NB, Graham R, Schmittling G: Entry of US medical school graduates into family practice residencies: 1991-1992 and 11-year summary. *Fam Med* 1992;24:504.

Kurtzke J et al: On the production of neurologists in the United States. *Neurology* 1991;41:1.

NRMP, *NRMP Data: March 1996*. Washington, DC: NRMP, 1996.

Slone R: Resident Selection. *Inv Rad* 1991;26:390.

Taylor C et al: The process of resident selection: A view from the residency director's desk. *Obstet Gynecol* 1995;85:299.

Getting Residency Information and Applications

WHERE CAN I LEARN ABOUT RESIDENCY PROGRAMS?

Before you start the application process, you will need to acquire enough information about the available residency programs to make a list of programs that fit your needs. Fortunately, there is no scarcity of data about training programs (Table 4–1). In fact, you will have to be selective and efficient in your information gathering. For example, career advisers can provide broad perspectives on a number of different programs, including clinical training and research. On the other hand, junior faculty, fellows and house staff can give you the nitty-gritty about training at an individual program, based on their residency experience. There is no one source that will tell everything as it relates to your goals.

Career Adviser

Your career adviser, whether a department chairperson or a junior faculty member, should be aware of the programs that best fit your personal and career goals. Your adviser should also be able to provide information not found in FREIDA to help you understand the "personality" of the program. For example, he or she should know whether the program currently has a department chair, what type of research is conducted at that institution, the academic and clinical foci of the program, and the program's overall reputation.

If you are in luck, or if your school has been a "pipeline" into a specific program, your adviser might also know recent graduates of your medical school in the program whom you can contact. You can also request copies of the Match results of the last three graduating classes from your medical school and make phone calls on your own.

YOU WILL HAVE TO LOOK HIGH AND LOW TO OBTAIN A BALANCED PICTURE.

TABLE 4–1. Information resources for residency programs.	
Source	**Contribution**
Career adviser (Department chairperson, clinical faculty)	To identify appropriate programs which to apply and inform you of the current status of the program.
Dean of students	To help you choose between specialties, pick an adviser, and assess overall competitiveness.
House staff	To provide perspective on training and residency life.
Fourth-year medical students	To summarize what's hot/what's not: tips and warnings for prospects in your specialty.
AMA Fellowship and Residency Interactive Database Access (AMA-FREIDA)	To provide current contact information for your target programs as well as detailed statistics.
Graduate Medical Education Directory (The "Green Book")	To provides contacts for residency programs. Next best thing to FREIDA.
NRMP Program Results: Listing of Filled and Unfilled Programs	To lists the programs that did not fill all their spots in the previous Match.
Transitional Year Program Directory (The "Purple Book")	To give detailed listings of transitional year programs.
Directories published by some specialties	To supplement or update information in FREIDA.

THE DEAN OF STUDENTS IS OFTEN AN OVERLOOKED RESOURCE.

Dean of Students

This may seem obvious, but it is surprising how many students will pass up the opportunity to make an appointment, perhaps fearing that the dean is "too busy" to speak with them or is absorbed with weightier matters. Don't hesitate to schedule an appointment; this faculty person can be an excellent resource of information, advice, and advocacy.

Even a brief meeting can provide inside information about the workings of the Match at your school, advance word on how and when the Dean's letter will be written, an early assessment of your academic progress as it might influence your specialty and program choice, and suggestions about who the "hot" advisers are. It is never too early to get some hints about strategies, both academic and personal. And remember, many a Dean of Students have gone through this process themselves, and often in the not too distant past.

Faculty and House Staff

Faculty in your desired specialty that you meet on your junior and senior clerkships can complement information provided by your career adviser. Talk to as many of these people as possible and understand their perspectives (eg, geographic, academic vs clinical, etc). Senior residents can share their sense of the job market and their own job-hunting experiences. In addition, junior faculty and fellows can shed light on the residency programs that trained them. House staff can also provide information on programs they knew as medical students. Although house staff are in the best position to describe training and life as a resident, their perspective is limited to their own program and does not necessarily apply to any others.

Senior Medical Students

After surviving their interviews and Match Day, graduating seniors are your best bet for practical application and interviewing tips. Debriefing some of these survivors will give you an additional "feel" for the application process and alert you to potential trouble spots. Most medical schools organize question- and-answer sessions with graduating seniors. Remember, though, that while the seniors have considerable "trench" experience, their perspectives are understandably limited when it comes to what programs might be best for you.

Fellowship and Residency Electronic Interactive Database Access (AMA-FREIDA)

AMA-FREIDA is an annually updated PC-based database of residency programs, produced by the American Medical Association. It has supplanted the *Graduate Medical Education Directory* (aka the "Green Book") as the most popular source of information on residency programs. FREIDA can usually be found in your medical library or student affairs office. FREIDA can search for programs by specialty, region and state, dividing an overwhelming amount of information on each program into nine manageable categories (Table 4–2). The "Custom Queue" function allows you to collect data on programs of interest in multiple specialties and states.

> FREIDA IS A SELF-REPORTING DATABASE; IT DOES NOT COMPARE OR EVALUATE PROGRAMS.

If a printer is attached to the computer, you can print out the program information in varying levels of detail and peruse it at home. If you have a computer at home, you can instead save the data on a diskette as a text file (and save some trees as well), view it on your home computer, and print out selected portions. The FREIDA user's guide is cryptic at best; for simplified how-to information, consult Table 4–3. FREIDA also allows you to print mailing labels from its database; however, the printing has an unconventional appearance, with unusual abbreviations and strange formatting.

There are a few things to remember about FREIDA. The information is often incomplete or outdated. Moreover, all information is provided by the programs themselves without being verified. Sometimes program directors choose not to answer certain questions that they feel are irrelevant or em-

---

TABLE 4–2. Information in FREIDA.

General program information
Educational environment
Work environment
Compensation and benefits
Clinical environment
Patient population
Medical benefits/institution features
Specialties in institution

TABLE 4–3. Idiot's Guide to FREIDA.

Follow these steps to collect contact and program information. Consult the Help option for more information by pressing "F1" at any time. Press "Esc" to go back to previous menus and screens.

1. At the screen titled "Select Specialty," select the specialty by entering a three digit code and pressing "Return." A list of specialties with codes is available by pressing "Tab."

2. At the screen titled "Select State/Region," select the state or region to search by typing in the state initials and pressing "Return." A list of state initials and regions is available by pressing "Tab."

3. At the screen titled "Program Selections Options Menu," press "3" followed by "Return" to activate the Custom Queue function.

4. Press "1" to browse programs in the specific specialty and state/region. Use arrow keys to scroll through the list of programs. Press the spacebar if you want to highlight a program for the Custom Queue (CQ). An asterisk will appear to the left of the program. You can highlight multiple programs on the list. When you are done, you can add these programs to the CQ by pressing the "Insert" key.

5. You are now back at the CQ function screen. The counter at the top of the screen lets you know how many programs you currently have in the CQ. If you want to add programs from other states/regions, press "Esc" twice to get to the screen "Select State/Region" and repeat steps 2–4. If you want to add programs from a different specialty, press "Esc" thrice to get the screen "Select Specialty" and repeat steps 1–4. Otherwise, go to step 6.

6. If you want to review program information, press "3" and follow instructions. To print program information or save it to diskette, press "5," FREIDA will then display the programs that you saved to CQ. Scroll through and highlight all programs you want printed/saved to diskette. Press "F10" to continue.

7. You are now presented with an array of printing options. Choose "6" and follow instructions if you want to print/save contact addresses to request applications. Avery #5162 laser labels are ideal but not necessary. You can also print the addresses out on plain paper and retype them on labels. Choose "1" and follow instructions if you want to print/save program information. When saving to diskette, specify both filename and destination drive (eg, "A:\PROGRAMS.TXT"). Now that wasn't so bad, was it?

barrassing. Some programs do not fill out questionnaires at all and are listed only by name. Lastly, keep in mind that as a self-reporting database, FREIDA does not evaluate or compare programs.

Graduate Medical Education Directory: The "Green Book"

The *Graduate Medical Education Directory* is an annually updated catalog of all training programs recognized by the Accreditation Council for Graduate Medical Education (ACGME). Despite its heft, the directory has very little information for each program other than the contact address and telephone number (Table 4–4).

TABLE 4–4. Information in "Green Book" program listing.
Program director's name, address, telephone number
Sponsoring institution
Other institutions with a major role in training
Number of training years
Total number of positions in program
Program ID number

The Green Book can be obtained at your office of student affairs or medical library. You can order your own copy by calling or writing:

American Medical Association
Order Department OP416795
PO Box 109050
Chicago, IL 60610-9050
(800) 621-8335

If you are an IMG with no convenient access to AMA-FREIDA, you should probably purchase your own copy of the Green Book. Although the program information contained in it is not as extensive as that in FREIDA, the Green Book does feature **some** facts not covered in FREIDA. These include visa and certification guidelines for foreign-born medical graduates seeking graduate medical education in the United States, detailed ACGME requirements for program accreditation by specialty (yawn), and state licensure requirements.

Transitional Year Program Directory: The "Purple Book"

The Purple Book lists most transitional year programs and includes contact information, information on required and elective rotations, call schedule, etc. Because much of the same data is available on AMA-FREIDA, use the Purple Book as a secondary resource. It should be available at your office of student affairs or medical library. A copy can be ordered by calling or writing:

Association for Hospital Medical Education
1200 19th Street NW, Suite 300
Washington, DC 20036-2401
(202) 857-1196

NRMP Program Results: Listing of Filled and Unfilled Programs

As described in Chapter 2, the *NRMP Program Results* lists all programs that did not fill their spots in the NRMP Match. If you are a weak candidate in a strong field, however, you might take a closer look at these programs. If not available at your student affairs office, the book can be ordered by calling or writing:

ATTN: Membership and Publication Orders
National Residency Matching Program
2450 N Street NW
Washington, DC 20037-1129
(202) 828-0416

BE WARY OF PROGRAMS WITH UNFILLED SPOTS IN COMPETITIVE SPECIALTIES.

Specialty-Specific Directories

Several specialties maintain directories of training programs with contact information. A handful of directories (including those from family practice, internal medicine, psychiatry, physical medicine and rehabilitation, and preventive medicine) rival or surpass FREIDA in terms of comprehensiveness and appropriateness of information. In general, though, the specialty directories are not updated as frequently as FREIDA or the "Green Book." See Chapter 3 for more information on directories that may be available in your specialty.

HOW MANY PROGRAMS SHOULD I APPLY TO?

Most students want enough applications to ensure a healthy number of interviews, which in turn helps to ensure a successful match. The number of programs you apply to depends on a number of factors, namely: (1) your competitive standing; (2) the competitiveness of the specialty; (3) the competitiveness of the programs to which you are applying; and (4) whether you're participating in the couples match.

Because several factors figure into the equation, it's best to settle on a number with the help of your career adviser. If, however, you are even mildly interested in a particular program, write or call for an information packet and application. If you remain unsure, err on the side of submitting too many applications. Don't worry about going overboard at this point. It is better to decline interview invitations later, rather than to realize that you do not have enough interviews to ensure a good match.

Consider the "Rule of Thirds" to achieve a balanced set of applications and minimize your chances of not matching. A third of your applications should go to your "dream programs" regardless of their competitiveness. Another third should include desirable programs where you have a solid chance of matching. The last third consists of acceptable programs that can serve as back ups. The Rule of Thirds works best in the less competitive specialties. See "Your Specialty and the Match" on page 19 to find the general prescription for the healthy number of applications in each field.

HOW DO I OBTAIN APPLICATIONS?

Requesting applications is the step that triggers an avalanche of paperwork. To keep yourself sane (and stable) during this process, **follow two rules from the start**: (1) Finalize your list of target programs before beginning the application process. Adding and dropping applications in midstream will mean having to track that much more paperwork; (2) Try to complete each step of

BETTER TO HAVE TOO MANY APPLICATIONS THAN TOO FEW.

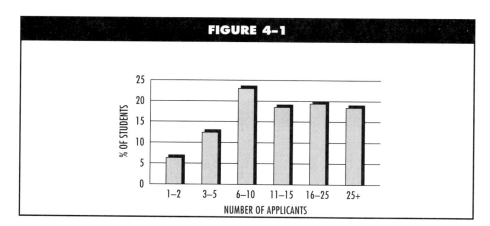

FIGURE 4-1

Number of residency applications made by U.S. fourth-year medical students.

FIGURE 4-2

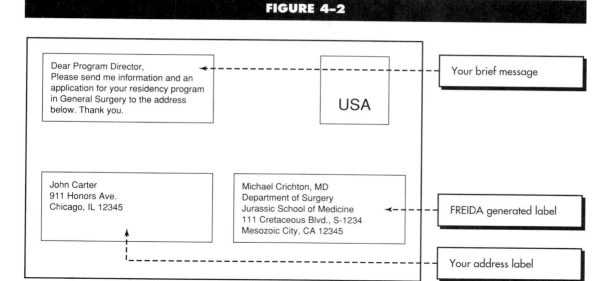

Sample application request postcard.

each application at the same time. For example, request at once all required transcripts.

To request applications, purchase pre-stamped postcards at the Post Office. If you're using a computer word processor, it's simple and worth the effort to create three sets of labels. On the first set, write a brief note requesting information and an application.

Type your address on the second set, and the name of the program director and the program addresses on the third set of labels. Then, simply attach the three labels to the face of the postcard in the appropriate spots (Figure 4–2).

You should send for applications and program information **no later than early August.** Allow 2 to 3 weeks to receive applications from programs, then follow up with phone calls as needed. If you fall behind time on requests, consider calling all the programs directly for information and applications. It's worth the cost of the phone calls and you might be able to get answers to some simple questions while requesting applications.

WHAT SHOULD I BE LOOKING FOR IN A PROGRAM?

Before you set up your list of programs to apply to, you need to have some idea of your priorities. You don't need crystal-ball clarity at this point, but it is necessary for you to think through the following issues rather early in the process. You should review the following issues when you start interviewing.

Location

Geography is a critical though highly personal issue. Some candidates are restricted by employment requirements of their significant other. Others want

TABLE 4–5. Some application hot spots.
Boston
Chicago
Hawaii
San Diego
San Francisco
Seattle

to be near family, or wish to use residency as an opportunity to establish contacts in the community in which ultimately they hope to practice. If you are adventurous and have no serious "attachments," then consider programs that will place you on new terrain. Many doing preliminary or transitional PGY-1 years take advantage of the chance to experience another city with limited commitment. It might be your last chance to do so before marital and family responsibilities catch up with you. In either case, recognize that even weak programs can be competitive if they have an attractive location (Table 4–5).

Most students acquire a sense of regional variations in styles and attitudes towards residency training. For example, many students who have trained on both coasts report that faculty tend to be less formal in the West Coast institutions. In the course of your interviews, you may pick up some regional flavors in the medical training available. Decide what suits your tastes.

Setting

Most applicants' career plans can be categorized as either academically oriented, clinically oriented, or both. You want to find a program that fits your preference. Many programs can be classified into the following settings: university, community, city/county, HMO, private or VA. Many of these programs run services at more than one hospital, thus offering their residents exposure to multiple settings. It's worth your while to ask about the amount of time you would spend at each hospital.

University: A university medical school affiliation is advantageous for two reasons: (1) medical schools offer teaching opportunities; and (2) the presence of medical students ensures a setting geared towards teaching the residents as well. Teaching conferences are generally of higher quality in university programs than in other settings. There are, however, a few drawbacks. For starters, university programs can be more intense, which tends to contribute to a lower level of sociability among the residents. Residents in university programs tend to have greater access to knowledgeable consultants but, some residents complain that because of this wealth of specialists and consultants, they have less autonomy and decision-making responsibility. Likewise, for better or worse, patient populations in a university setting are often not representative of what the resident will encounter in community practice after training. The plus is that university programs tend to be based in tertiary care centers that give their residents exposure to the more unusual or interesting cases.

Urban/county: If you really want hands-on experience, city and county hospitals will virtually give you blisters. You can forget academic theorization here; you'll be taught to manage a large patient volume: a population largely consisting of urban poor. Most likely, you will be heavily involved in the decision-making process and will gain more experience with a variety of invasive procedures. Unfortunately, at a county or city hospital you are frequently overworked and underpaid. These programs often lack the academic prestige and name-recognition of their university equivalents, with notable exceptions such as Massachusetts General Hospital. In addition, ancillary support tends to be weaker, and formal teaching is often uneven and disorganized.

FIGURE 4-3A

Program Name _____

Date of Visit _____

Factor	Comments
Location	
Setting	
Reputation	
Stability of program	
Subspecialty strengths	
Education	
Conferences/rounds	
Faculty teaching	
Post-residency plans of graduates	
Research/teaching opportunities	
Work environment	
Patient population/load	
Patient responsibilities	
Call frequency/ hours per week	
Ancillary support (eg, nursing)	
On call support (eg, nightfloat, admission caps)	
Health benefits	
Non-health benefits	
Vacation/sick leave/ parenting leave	

Program evaluation worksheet (PEW).

FIGURE 4-3B

Other Factors/Notes

Gut feeling

Advantages	Disadvantages

Preliminary Rank

☐ Top third ☐ Middle third ☐ Bottom third ☐ Do not rank

Interview Log

Name/Address	Notes

Community: Residents usually receive kinder, gentler training at a community program. Salaries and benefits also tend to be more humane. Because there is less academic pressure, residents are typically more relaxed and have more time for reading. However, well-organized rounds and conferences may be lacking. Like city and county programs, community programs are academically less prestigious. Given the large proportion of private patients and private attendings, you may not receive the same degree of patient responsibility or experience with certain procedures.

Stability

With graduate medical education facing drastic cuts in federal funding, you should determine how financially secure a residency program is. How much of its funding comes from federal sources? How well off is the parent hospital or university?

In addition, many teaching hospitals (especially on the East and West Coasts) are now experiencing unprecedented competition from managed care. Does the parent hospital enjoy a robust patient base, or is it floundering in a rising tide of managed care?

Reputation

A program's reputation invariably comes into play if the applicant is considering fellowship training or a career in academic medicine. Its reputation, whether deserved or not, can visibly influence your ability to secure competitive fellowships or faculty appointments in the future. However, if the program is too large, no matter how prestigious, you may have to sweat to get the strong personal recommendations necessary to secure a competitive fellowship. The reality in community practice is that most patients will not know or really care what medical school you graduated from, much less where you trained.

Subspecialty Strengths

If you're considering subspecialty training after residency, you might reevaluate programs with strengths in that subspecialty. In addition, it never hurts to have a well-known "name" in a subspecialty write you a strong letter of recommendation.

Educational Environment

Because residency programs are a form of post-graduate education, you need to appraise the educational philosophy and facilities at the institutions that interest you. Pay attention to the following aspects of residency programs:

Curriculum/conferences: Residents depend on well-organized conferences and teaching rounds to expand their knowledge base and reinforce what they already know. Most programs have, or are developing, an organized required curriculum that exposes residents to all major topics in the specialty during their training. The curriculum might include rotations, conferences, and syllabi with assigned reading. In some specialties, there is a lot of variation in emphasis and formality; **you** have to decide which combination best fits your needs. For example, some family practice programs emphasize obstetrics; others practically exclude it. Some medicine programs feature heavy experience and training in HIV; others have next to none.

Faculty teaching: The teaching that residents receive from faculty, and the rapports they establish with them can be correlated to a number of factors:

faculty-to-resident ratio, program setting, proportion of private attendings, and overall size of the program. A large program cannot provide as much personal mentoring, but thankfully you are less at the mercy of a few quirky personalities. When you visit the program, get a sense of what interest the faculty maintains in the training and welfare of its house staff. What type of feedback does the house staff receive from the faculty? Is there a mechanism for evaluation of the faculty?

Research and teaching opportunities: While research and teaching opportunities are nearly essential for those planning on an academic career or subspecialty training, they are also desirable even if you have no plans of staying within academic walls. When you assess the research opportunities at a program, ask yourself the following questions. Are there well-established researchers available to guide residents? Is there time allotted for research, either as a requirement or as an elective? How successful is the program in securing grants, hospital funding or internal funding for research? How satisfied are the residents who are presently completing their projects? Or, for that matter, how many dissatisfied residents will cite a lack of institutional financial support?

Work Environment

Don't forget to survey the working environment when you size up a residency program. After all, you'll be putting in a lot of hours in that set of buildings with their cast of characters. So don't overlook these considerations:

Work versus education: Many programs are guilty of exploiting the "cheap labor" of residents without providing a rich educational experience. Residency is "learning by doing" to be sure, but be on the lookout for how service versus education is balanced.

Patient population/load: The optimal patient load will provide you with enough clinical experience and will leave you with adequate time and energy to read and attend teaching conferences. Patient load is often a function of the program's setting (see above). On your interview visits, ask for an average patient census, and discreetly ask residents how they feel about the workload. Know what medical problems are common in the population served by the program. For example, an orthopedics program may get more than its share of trauma cases because of its location near several major highways. In addition, you want to get a feel for other characteristics of the patient population, such as ethnicity/language (a large Spanish-speaking population?), socioeconomic status (urban poor?), and attitude (typical Saturday night ER crowd?). Keep in mind that the best training environment does not have to match that of your future practice.

Patient responsibilities: The whole point of residency training is to provide you with the experience and skills necessary for you to practice medicine unsupervised. When you visit the program, find out if the attending allows the resident to "run the show," or if the resident needs approval for major decisions. Next, is backup assistance readily available if the resident or intern needs help? Or are you on your own even if World War III breaks out on your watch?

Call schedule: Call schedules vary widely by specialty, setting, year of training, and training site (for programs with multiple sites). Recognize the range of calls that can deprive you of a good night's sleep (Table 4–6). The house officer will often encounter a mix of calls during the year. How much

ONE SURGICAL RESIDENT TO ANOTHER. . . .
Q: WHAT'S WRONG WITH EVERY-OTHER-NIGHT CALL?
A: YOU MISS OUT ON HALF THE GOOD CASES.

TABLE 4–6. Types of calls.		
Type	**Description**	**Ask About**
Long call	House officer admits patients throughout a 24-hour period. Sometimes there is a nightfloat that takes admissions after a certain hour and cross-cover that assists a team if a member has clinic that day.	How many admissions per night, how much sleep intern/resident typically gets, and whether there is a nightfloat or cross-cover.
Short call	House officer takes admissions from morning until a certain hour at night.	When short call ends and if there is an admissions cap.
Home/beeper call	House officer is on call outside hospital. How often the resident comes into the hospital depends on nature of admission or issue of current patient; and if other members of the team are in hospital.	How often intern/resident comes into hospital.
Jeopardy call	House officer can be placed on call on short notice to cover for sick colleague or to alleviate heavy patient admissions. Usually used on otherwise light or no call rotations.	
Nightfloat	House officer on a dedicated night rotation takes admissions for on-call team after a certain time (i.e., midnight). Admissions are transferred to another team in the morning.	How many weeks are you on nightfloat, and at what time nightfloat duties start.

sleep you typically get during a call night and how late you work post-call is almost as important as how often you're on call. For many specialties, call frequency often varies by training year.

Closely tied to call schedule is the number of work hours per week, information available on FREIDA. Know your own threshold and the workload you are willing to tolerate.

Ancillary support: No one is an island, and your team certainly doesn't go it alone in caring for your patients. Good nursing support, consulting services, phlebotomy, laboratory, hospital information services, transport services and emergency room care are keys to a smooth clinical work experience. As an intern, you will often be used as a person of last resort to fill any gaps in ancillary support (unless you scut the poor medical student).

Esprit de corps: *Esprit de corps* is a familiar, albeit foreign, term for morale. Trust your intuition as well as your powers of observation. Are the residents "happy campers"? Is the atmosphere friendly or competitive? What kind of camaraderie exists among the residents? Among faculty, house staff, and administration? Look for the answers on your visit by asking the house staff and ancillary staff. Quietly divide and conquer. It is usually easier to get an honest answer in private from a departing resident than the chief resident or the program director in front of 20 other interviewees. Afterwards, assess the quality of your own experience during the visit.

DON'T FORGET TO ASK HOW MUCH SLEEP YOU GET WHEN ON CALL AND ABOUT THE LENGTH OF THE POST-CALL DAY.

WHAT RESIDENTS DO NOT SAY MAY BE MORE TELLING THAN WHAT THEY DO SAY.

Salary

Residents are paid so little that salary is usually not the central issue. Interestingly enough, most of your paycheck comes from the federal government rather than the program itself: thus, you may be fattening the bottom line of a hospital that is not even paying you. The average income of an intern in 1994–95 was $30,573. Don't bother calculating your pay per hour; it will only depress you. Salary information is readily available on FREIDA. Your income usually rises incrementally during your residency training, but not by much. It is critical to factor in cost of living when comparing salaries: $28,000 will take you much further in Louisville, Kentucky, than $32,000 in Los Angeles (Table 4–7).

For many, these low figures are reason enough to moonlight. Once licensed to practice medicine (typically, after the first year), you can usually earn anywhere from $20 to $120 per hour working in a variety of settings, including emergency rooms, nursing homes, outpatient clinics (ie, "doc in the box"); doing insurance company physical exams; and even working in prisons. Some programs actually provide in-house moonlighting opportunities which can be a major source of supplementary income. In-house jobs will often take into account your regular call schedule, making it easier to moonlight during residency. On the other hand, many programs officially ban moonlighting or actively discourage it, so tactfully ask about it on your visit, and someone (usually a graduating resident) will give you the scoop.

IN-HOUSE MOONLIGHTING OFFERS THE BEST OF BOTH WORLDS.

Benefits

Though everyone remembers salary, don't forget the benefits. Many programs offer medical insurance, dental services, paid drug prescriptions, employee health services, and psychiatric counseling (Table 4–8). Shop around carefully, especially if you have a family. Be aware that certain benefits at some programs are only available if the resident pays a portion of the cost. You don't want to end up spending part of your meager salary for benefits that other programs would have provided for free. When evaluating insurance, ask yourself: (1) who is covered (ie, family); (2) what is covered; (3) what costs do I pay out of pocket?

KEY BENEFITS = $$$

TABLE 4–7. Average 1994 stipends					
Year	All	Northeast	South	Midwest	West
PGY-1	$30,753	$33,102	$28,715	$30,290	$28,610
PGY-2	32,331	36,868	29,815	31,486	31,614
PGY-3	33,928	36,868	31,001	32,757	33,925
PGY-4	35,488	38,579	32,303	34,063	36,053
PGY-5	36,929	40,286	33,598	35,341	37,941
PGY-6	38,258	41,947	34,748	36,427	39,998

TABLE 4-8. Survey of health benefits offered by residency programs.				
Benefit	% Fully Paid (Resident/ Family)	% Offered/Cost Shared (Resident/Family)	% Offered/Not Paid (Resident/Family)	% Not Available (Resident/ Family)
Group medical insurance	59/42	40/53	0/6	1/1
Group dental insurance	47/34	33/40	13/18	7/8
Vision	34/27	28/35	8/9	31/28
Drug prescriptions	52/42	42/50	2/3	4/5
Psychiatric benefits	59/47	37/44	1/5	2/4
Counseling	59/49	34/38	2/4	6/9

In addition to health benefits, you want to ensure that your program offers adequate life, disability, and liability insurance. After 4 years in medical school and untold thousands of dollars, you (and your family) don't want to be left high and dry if you get sick, have an accident, or something else goes wrong. If you're planning on starting a family during residency training, then scrutinize the rules on maternity/paternity leave (Table 4–9). Find out if the policy is written or if it varies with each case (and personality). Of course, to date maternity leave policies tend to be more generous than paternity leave policies.

Other benefits to consider include parking, housing, meals, vacation, education leave for conferences, library services (eg, photocopying), and child care (Table 4–10).

HOW DO I ORGANIZE THIS INFORMATION?

Great. You know what to look for. But now you need to be able to organize and evaluate all the data. You are already receiving information from multiple sources: FREIDA, your adviser, and house officers at your medical institution. You will be flooded with more information on your visits to the programs. We've included a Program Evaluation Worksheet (PEW) which will allow you to organize information conveniently and evaluate a program ob-

TABLE 4-9. Issues addressed by a complete parental leave policy.
Duration of leaves allowed before and after delivery
Which category of leave credited
Whether leave is paid or unpaid
Whether provision is made for continuation of insurance benefits and the payment of premiums
Whether sick leave and vacation time may be accrued from year to year or used in advance
Whether make-up time will be paid
Policies for adoption
Whether schedule accommodations are allowed

TABLE 4–10. Survey of non-health benefits offered by residency programs.				
Benefit	% Fully Paid	% Offered/ Cost Shared	% Offered/ Not Paid	% Not Available
Life insurance	82	11	3	5
Disability insurance	77	5	6	13
Housing	53	11	14	71
Parking	61	15	20	4
Meals at work	23	28	24	26
Meals while on call	84	11	1	4

jectively (Figures 4–3A and 4–3B). Make a copy for each program on your application hit list. Take them with you on the interview trail to record notes and impressions.

REFERENCES

Association of American Medical Colleges: COTH Survey of House Staff Stipends, Benefits and Funding, 1994. Washington, DC, 1994.

Bickel J: Maternity leave policies for residents: An overview of issues and problems. Acad Med 1989;64:498.

Reiss G: A guide to obtaining postgraduate medical training. Resident & Staff Physician 1982; p. 111.

The Application

WHAT IS IN AN APPLICATION?

By August, brochures and applications from the programs of your choice should start pouring in. A complete program application file consists of several documents or sets of documents that you must assemble, track, and finally send off. You will be pulling together its components all summer and into early fall (Table 5–1). If you don't already own a file drawer or document storage box, buy a set of hanging file folders or an accordion file, and a set of manila file folders to organize your materials. They're an inexpensive investment in protecting your paperwork from late-night coffee spills, and protecting **you** from the potential embarrassment of sending Program X's forms to Program Y.

HOW DO I ORGANIZE THE PAPERWORK?

As you read through each application packet, you will notice that each program has its own set of application requirements. These requirements are outlined in the program's cover letter, or within the application itself. Some will ask you to complete the NRMP Universal Application; others will include their own forms. Some programs want your undergraduate transcript in addition to your medical school transcript. To help you keep track of who wants what, photocopy enough copies of the enclosed Worksheet for Application Requirements (WAR) to list all the programs that you are applying to (Figure 5–1).

Remember that in order to keep paperwork from escalating out of control: (1) do not add any new programs to your list after you have started work on the applications; and (2) try to complete 1 item (eg, transcript obtaining) for all applications at the same time.

FOR MAXIMUM EFFICIENCY AND MINIMUM CONFUSION, ORGANIZE APPLICATION REQUIREMENTS ON A WORKSHEET (LIKE OURS).

WHO EVALUATES MY APPLICATION?

As you assemble your application materials, remember your audience. The residency selection committee is usually composed of the residency director, several faculty members, and a few house officers. They are **extremely busy people**, and would rather be doing something other than screening your ap-

THE BUSIER THE SELECTION COMMITTEE, THE MORE LITTLE THINGS WILL BOTHER THEM.

TABLE 5-1. Common elements of an application file.		
Document	**Function**	**Quick advice**
Program application	Foundation of application file	Request by early August. Better to get too many than too few
Dean's letter	Compendium of written evaluations compiled by Dean of Student Affairs	Take an active role in helping Dean by editing/supplementing content if possible. Clarify any inaccuracies
Letters of recommendation	Written testimonials from faculty familiar with your work	Solicit letters no later than August. Confirm that writer feels comfortable writing a "strong" letter
Transcript	Academic record	Proofread an unofficial copy before having them sent out
CV	Summary of your credentials, activities and accomplishments	Pull together by July. Nice to have for personal statement and to accompany requests for letters of recommendation
Personal statement	Opportunity to establish your own voice and distinguish yourself from other applicants	Finish personal statement before applications arrive. Multiple reviewers and revisions are key

plication on a Saturday afternoon. Make their job as pleasant as possible by having a neat, professional-looking application with clear, succinct answers.

Remember that in addition to the faculty, departmental or administrative assistants can make or break an application. The comments they provide the committee on their interactions with you may well color the committee's initial impressions. If the departmental secretary likes you well enough, he or she may actually push for your application or direct it to a receptive committee member. If you miss any deadlines, friendly administrative assistants may bend rules to keep your application in the running. If anything goes wrong in your application, you will need every ally you can get.

HOW DO THEY EVALUATE MY APPLICATION?

Once your application arrives on the desk of the program director, he or she will direct its contents to a number of different readers at different phases in the evaluation process. The typical process can be divided into several stages, which we will outline for you.

Screening

In the initial phase of the evaluation process, your application is usually screened by a select few overworked committee members after hours during the week or during weekend afternoons. Screeners will read your application, the letters of recommendation, selected portions of the dean's letter, and the transcript. When they look at the dean's letter, committee members typically focus on junior and senior clerkship evaluations in their field, and scan the summary paragraph for the crucial code words (See Table 5–4). Note that the personal statement tends to carry little or no weight at this point in the process, since the screener has another 50 files or so to plow through. The screener then completes an evaluation form, which will toss

THE PROGRAM SECRETARY CAN BE A POWERFUL ALLY.

FIGURE 5-1

Directions: Fill in blanks below of requested numbers/names/dates. Under **Application Requirements**, list each requirement by name. Once you have assembled the item for that application, check it off.

Program Name	Application Mailing Address	Contact & Phone #	App. Deadline	Application Requirements		Notes
				☐	☐	
				☐	☐	
				☐	☐	
				☐	☐	
				☐	☐	
				☐	☐	
				☐	☐	
				☐	☐	
				☐	☐	
				☐	☐	
				☐	☐	
				☐	☐	
				☐	☐	
				☐	☐	
				☐	☐	
				☐	☐	
				☐	☐	
				☐	☐	
				☐	☐	
				☐	☐	
				☐	☐	
				☐	☐	
				☐	☐	
				☐	☐	
				☐	☐	

Worksheet for application requirements.

your application into one of three piles: a recommendation to interview, maybe interview, or not interview. Some programs grant interviews on a rolling basis, so again it's best to get your application in as early as possible.

The Interview

Many conscientious interviewers will review your file before the actual interview. Others will prefer to review the file while you're sitting there in their office, which can be distracting to you when you're already under stress. Busy interviewers zoom in on areas that consistently give the most information bang for the buck, like the CV, transcript, letters of recommendation from "known" writers, and the Dean's letter. The importance of your personal statement will depend on the individual interviewer and the specialty.

Ranking Sessions

After all the interviews have been completed, there is at least one highly charged, exhausting session in which the full committee attempts to rank the candidates they've seen. In many cases, not all applicants interviewed are ranked. The real committee battles are **not** fought over the names high on the rank list. The top applicants are easy to rank. Rather, the committee members will squabble over the names in the middle ground. As you might expect, the battle heats up near the rank spot to which they had to drop last year to fill their program (if they filled at all) (Figure 5–2).

As the meeting wears on, the application files are usually subjected to closer scrutiny. At this point, the committee is likely to overanalyze your personal statement. Anything unusual in your personal statement (eg, a description of the grunge band that you hope to organize during your residency) or the rest of your application is much more likely to be judged bizarre than as a factor weighted in your favor. Bottom line: be smart, assertive, yet conservative in tone and approach—that is, don't take unnecessary chances.

Selection Factors

Throughout the evaluation process, the selection committee tests its pool of

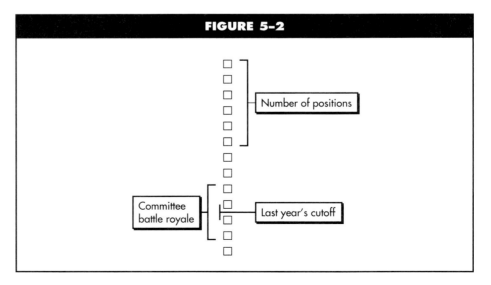

FIGURE 5-2

Number of positions

Committee battle royale

Last year's cutoff

Where most battles are fought on the rank list.

applicants against certain criteria important to its program. You may think that all programs want is an applicant elected to AΩA, spectacular board scores, and "Honors" plastered all over the transcript. However, academic standing is only part of the story. What good is stellar academic performance if the applicant does not interact smoothly with current faculty, house staff and administration? Program directors want residents who work hard and perform well as part of a team. According to the program directors themselves, the factors most important to residency committees tend to be personal (Table 5–2).

Of course, overall academic performance is still important. Among the major academic selection factors, grades in the specialty rotation and electives seem to be the most crucial (Figure 5–3). Bear in mind that the significance of these academic factors varies from specialty to specialty. For example, psychiatry residency directors rate AΩA membership as "somewhat important," whereas general surgery residency directors consider this honor as a "very important" academic selection factor. See Chapter 3, "Your Specialty and the Match," to find out the key criteria in your specialty.

PROGRAM APPLICATIONS

The NRMP Universal Application was created to simplify the application

TABLE 5-2. Factors most important to program directors.
1. Attitude
2. Stability
3. Interpersonal skills
4. Academic performance
5. Maturity

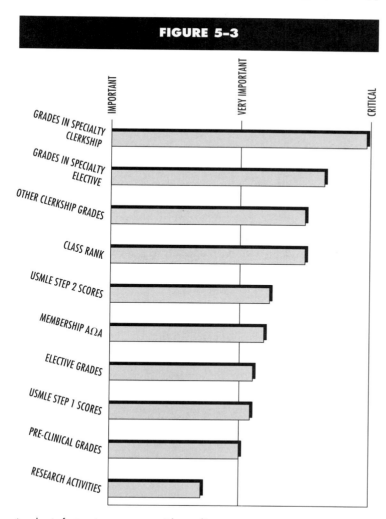

FIGURE 5–3

Academic factors important to residency directors.

process. The idea was that you would complete this application only once, and then send photocopies of the application to programs that accept it. Unfortunately, programs that accept the Universal Application are in the minority. The majority of programs insist on using their own forms. The writing process can be very frustrating since these "custom" applications often differ only slightly from the Universal Application in content, but use unique layouts, forcing the applicant back to his or her typewriter/word processor for yet another round of cut-and-paste.

If any of your prospective programs request the Universal Application, **fill it out first**. Much of the material that it calls for will resurface in other application forms. Some students find it helpful to hire a secretarial service to handle the paperwork and produce top-quality customized application materials. If you are on busy clinical rotations, or don't have the skills or compulsiveness to track all the details yourself, these services can be a sanity preserver.

When you receive a program application, **make at least two photocopies**. Write the necessary information by hand neatly on one of the photocopies before typing on the original. If you mortally mess up the original and have no time to request another, the second photocopy serves as a backup. As you complete the applications, keep the following tips in mind:

▶ For information to be filled in on the form itself, use a good electric typewriter with perfect error correction. Or, if you are experienced and ambitious, use a word processor. This second method involves the risky process of feeding applications into laser printers or photocopiers (the overlay method)—a test of your alignment skills. Word processing is best reserved for the personal statement, where looks count and a nice, proportionally-spaced computer font is more compact and readable than most typewriter fonts. If you can't do it right, get help from a computer-savvy friend or a secretarial service.

▶ Avoid filling a blank on an application with "See CV" or "See Personal Statement". These abbreviations may make sense to you, but they can annoy residency directors to no end, since the personal statement or CV is often a loose piece of paper elsewhere in your application file. In addition, these shorthand terms bespeak a certain lack of motivation. You can, of course, abbreviate specific titles or similar terms in the information requested if necessary (eg, "U" for "University," "Schl" for "School," etc.) If the space provided is too small, fill it in with the most important information; **only then** add "Also see CV" or "Also see Personal Statement."

▶ When you are finished, **make and file a photocopy of the complete application**. Applications do get lost in the mail, and you might need to fax or send a replacement by express mail to the program if the Post Office fouls up. Also, having your copy handy right before your interview is a helpful memory refresher. Reviewing what you wrote in your application will help you anticipate questions and avoid possible inconsistencies between what you put down on paper and what you say in person.

If a program high on your list gives you the choice of the NRMP Universal Application or their own form, use their form and resist the urge to take the easy way out, especially if they indicate preference for their form.

GIVE THEM WHAT THEY ASK FOR WHERE THEY WANT IT.

THE DEAN'S LETTER

As we mentioned earlier, the letter from your dean is a key item at the screening and interview stages of the application process. Deans' letters convey a variety of different types of information about you to discerning committee members (Figure 5–4). Although the dean's letter is supposed to be an objective evaluation of your medical school performance, most Deans' letters come across as enthusiastic letters of recommendation, thus bolstering many average or weaker applicants, but possibly diluting the very strong ones.

FIGURE 5-4

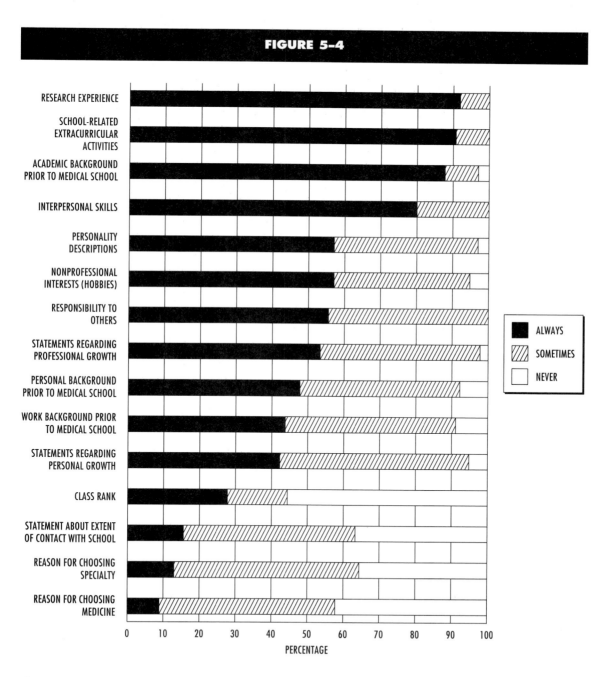

Information that commonly appears in deans' letters.

Though deans' letters can vary a lot, they typically contain the following components:

- **Personal background information.** This includes pertinent and noteworthy information from your undergraduate career and medical school application (eg, graduating *magna cum laude*, leadership positions, etc.).

- **Pre-clinical evaluations.** This section will tell the committee about your preclinical honors; or, on the other hand, about any irregularities in progress or required remediation.

- **Clinical evaluations.** Typically the longest portion of the Dean's letter. The majority of letters will include quotes from your clinical evaluations. Some letters cite the evaluations verbatim, others use abridged versions or just choice excerpts. Some Deans' letters include histograms depicting the grade distributions in courses and rotations, and marking the student's position on each histogram.

- **Special activities.** Here the Dean has an opportunity to highlight your extracurricular activities and any outstanding achievements. These passages often read like portraiture or—at worst—caricature.

- **Summary paragraph.** This section is usually read first by the residency selection committee. It is typically a concise synopsis of the Dean's letter, and likewise often provides a comparative analysis of your performance, whether through a class rank, class percentile or buzzwords that function to cluster or single out students (Table 5–3).

KNOW WHAT INFLUENCE YOU HAVE OVER YOUR DEAN'S LETTER.

The letter can be written without your input. At the other extreme, your school might ask you to proofread the letter for typos and factual errors, or even allow you limited editorial privileges with regard to the content. Other schools will consider it a federal offense if you so much as sneak a peek at your Dean's letter. If the Dean's office calls you in for a talk with the Dean, be sure to bring along your CV or personal statement. In any event, ask savvy seniors and your student affairs office about the structure of the typical dean's letter from your institution, and what role you can expect to play in its final form. Table 5–4 presents a tongue-in-cheek view of the code words found in the dean's letter.

If you have the opportunity to review your Dean's letter, check it carefully for accuracy, grammar, and spelling, and for the presence of all your clerkship evaluations (no need to point out any weak ones that might be missing). If you have not already done so, do not hesitate to visit your Dean of Students to discuss any evaluations that you believe to be unfair, inaccurate or even malicious. If your school gives you the opportunity to edit the content of your dean's letter, **grab it!** Medical schools want their graduates to do well, and few can market you like you yourself. Make sure the dean's letter emphasizes your strong points in detail, while tactfully expressing con-

TABLE 5-3. Examples of buzz words used in Deans' letters.		
Recommend in highest terms	Outstanding	Strongest of year
Recommend very highly	Excellent	Very strong
Recommend highly	Very good	Strong
Recommend	Good	Good

Best → Worst

TABLE 5-4. The unofficial guide to translating the Dean's letter[1]	
What the Dean Says	**What the Dean Really Means**
Sensitive	Cries easily
Very sensitive	Cries on rounds
Very cooperative	Easy; will work extra nights
Relatively good	Wouldn't want him/her for my doctor
Sensitive to patients' needs	Steals food from their trays
Extremely capable	A little better than average
Well-liked	His/her mom always spoke well of him/her
Extremely conscientious	Probably paranoid
Assertive	A real SOB
Self-motivated	Obnoxious
Outstanding integrity	On parole; is watching every step
Enthusiastic	Hebephrenic
Grasps new concepts quickly	Basically stupid, but flexible
Highly satisfactory	Extremely average
Compulsive, goal-oriented	Obnoxious, but no more than average
Recommend with confidence	Glad to get him/her out of our school
Recommend with reservation	Glad to get him/her out of our school
Look forward to watching this individual mature in his/her career	Sure hope the fool improves
Will be an asset to your program	Don't call us, we'll call you!

[1] Adapted, with permission, from the *New England Journal of Medicine*.

cerns about negative material that may have made its way into the collection. Everyone has suffered a premature or harsh judgment made by someone who doesn't really know them. If you have one or two isolated "pans" in your record, a sympathetic Dean may be willing to soften or delete them.

Most deans' letters are mailed out on the first of November, a date agreed upon by the council of deans. A few send out their information earlier. For this reason, it's a good idea to confirm your Dean's mailing date. Then, provide your dean's office with your list of programs with addresses (as well as stamps and envelopes if necessary) **well before the mailing date.** Check with the office a day after the mailing date to confirm that your letters have indeed been sent.

LETTERS OF RECOMMENDATION

Along with your deans' letter, your letters of recommendation are vital to the success of your application. Take the time to select your letter writers wisely, and provide them with the materials they may need to refresh their memories when they write their recommendations.

When Should I Start Requesting Letters of Recommendation?
You can ask for letters after completing any significant clinical or research experience. Most students start collecting letters during the third year of

medical school. If you did well on a third-year clerkship, ask the attending to write a letter and put it aside while you are still fresh in his or her mind, keeping in mind that the letter can be modified later to reflect your specialty choice and career goals. In general, whenever you ask for a letter, give the writer at least 4 weeks to write the letter and mail it off.

How Do I Get a Strong Letter of Recommendation?

When you solicit letters of recommendation, there are a few steps you can take to maximize your chances of getting the strongest possible letters. First, go to the clerkship office and read the evaluations that your potential reference wrote about you during your rotation. The strength and eloquence of the writer's evaluation will certainly be reflected in any later letter written on your behalf.

Second, when asking for a letter of recommendation, phrase your request carefully. This precaution may reduce your vulnerability to weak letters. Tact and discretion are all the more important late in the game when clerkship evaluations may not be available to you. You can, for example, ask the person, "Do you think you know me well enough to write me a **strong** letter of recommendation?" If the potential referee does not feel comfortable writing you a strong letter, he or she can take the graceful exit you provided, saying, "Actually, I don't believe I know you well enough. Perhaps you should ask someone else." Then you are free to request a letter from another attending or faculty member who may provide you with a better reference.

Third, meet in person with the writer **before** he or she sits down to compose the letter, in order to discuss your choice of specialty and your career goals. Provide your letter writer with a copy of your personal statement, your CV, the names and addresses of the programs to which you are applying, (or a computer diskette, if the writer wants to do a mail merge), a set of stamps, and possibly a copy of their earlier evaluation of you if the comments were impressive and you would not mind having them recycled in the letter.

Some attendings will draft a letter of recommendation and offer you the chance to read it and either decline or accept it. If the letter is not as strong as you had hoped, you may decline it as long as you have better letters coming (Table 5–5). If the attending does not offer to show it to you, you may tactfully try the direct approach and ask if they would mind if you saw the letter or be less direct and ask to have a copy for your files. Many writers

PREPPING FOR RECOMMENDATION: ALWAYS MEET WITH YOUR WRITERS IN PERSON TO DISCUSS THEIR LETTERS.

ASK LETTER WRITERS TO SEND A COPY TO THE DEAN'S OFFICE TO HAVE READY IN CASE YOU MUST ENTER THE SCRAMBLE.

TABLE 5-5. Signs of a strong or weak letter.	
Strong	**Weak**
Typewritten on official letterhead and personally signed	Handwritten on plain paper and photocopied
Handwritten postscript with political schmoozing a big plus	Signed by an assistant or signature photocopied
Lengthy	Short
Detailed description of fund of knowledge, clinical skill, and past performance	Vague. Focuses on marginally relevant personality traits or work habits (eg, "He was punctual and well dressed.")
Frequent personal references	Lack of familiarity
Unconditional praise	Lukewarm praise; qualifications of any kind (*but, except,* etc.)

view this as a reasonable request since letters of recommendation often get lost and you may end up faxing a copy of the missing letter to the program to complete your file. If you are applying in a competitive specialty or you are a marginal candidate, then you may want copies of your letters of recommendation handy for the Scramble in case you do not match. Others still maintain that their letters should be strictly confidential. If you see the letter early and the letter is unfavorable (Table 5–5), you may decide to withhold program addresses. However, make sure you have someone else to go to for a letter. Even if letters have been sent, you should be aware of the content of the letters just in case it pops up during the residency interview.

Whom Should I Ask for Letters of Recommendation?

You should look for the following characteristics in all your letter writers if possible. He or she should be someone who:

▶ Will write you a strong letter

▶ Knows you well in a clinical setting

▶ Is well-established in the field (in order of desirability: chairman, professor, clinical instructor)

▶ Works in your specialty choice or in a related field

▶ Trained at or is well-known at your top-choice program.

If given the choice of a letter from a well-connected figure who does **not** know you well, or from a lesser-known attending who is familiar with you and your work, give priority to the person who knows you better. Unfortunately, many students request letters from less than optimal sources (Table 5–6). Letters from research mentors are acceptable if you already have two clinical letters and you have a strong interest in doing research in the future. Make sure it's from someone with whom you have done considerable work (ie, more than one summer). Letter selection also depends on the type of program you are applying to. It borders on excessive, but some applicants actually pick and choose from among 5 or more letter writers, depending upon the characteristics of each program on their list.

TRANSCRIPTS

Before you have your transcripts (medical school, and in some cases, undergraduate) mailed out, request some student copies to review for errors and completeness. Try to get your transcript requests to the Registrar's Office a few weeks before you send out your applications (September for most NRMP applicants). If you should receive additional excellent grades after the transcripts are mailed, send out updated transcripts.

PHOTO

Most applications reserve a space for a passport size photograph. Others will ask you to bring a photo when you interview. Though it is illegal to require a photograph with the application, it is better to comply unless you bear a striking resemblance to Darth Vader. Consider going to a studio for professional photography, and have color prints developed unless specified other-

TABLE 5-6. Sub-optimal sources for letters of recommendation.

Residents
Preclinical professors
Family, friends
Community figures
Previous employers

DON'T FORGET TO PROOFREAD YOUR TRANSCRIPT.

wise. If the pictures turn out well, you can send a 5x7 copy to your parents or your significant other.

APPLICATION COMPLETE POSTCARD

Residency programs have a variety of methods for acknowledging receipt of your application material, ranging from no response to a letter acknowledging receipt of the application form which checks any missing materials. Overall, it's up to you to track your application materials. This can easily be done by including a stamped, self-addressed postcard that notes receipt of your application and has a checklist for missing material (Figure 5–5). For the acknowledgment postcard to do its job, make sure that arrangements for all other materials are made well before sending in your applications. The exception is the Dean's letter, which is usually mailed out November 1.

Alternative Methods of Application Tracking. Unfortunately, the enclosed postcard only works if the overworked program secretary is in a mood to mail it back. Return receipt service available from the post office or express mail with tracking numbers are better but more expensive ways of tracking your applications. If you prefer, wait a few weeks after your application has been sent in, then call the program to check on your file (especially if you did not receive an application completed postcard). Not only will the contact person at the program verify if your file is complete, he or she may have advance word on your interview status. Most programs don't mind a phone call, as long as your manner is courteous and professional. Remember: the impression you make on the office staff may tip the balance toward or against your application.

APPLICATION "RECEIVED" DOES NOT EQUAL APPLICATION "COMPLETE." CONFIRM BY MAIL OR PHONE THAT ALL APPLICATIONS ARE COMPLETE WELL IN ADVANCE OF INTERVIEWS.

FIGURE 5-5

This is to acknowledge receipt of your application.

___ Your application is **complete.**

___ Your application is **not** complete. We are missing the following item(s):

___ Dean's letter
___ Transcript
___ Letter from Dr. Alpha
___ Letter from Dr. Beta
___ Letter from Dr. Gamma
___ Other _____

_____ _____
(You fill in the blank)
Program   Date

Sample application status postcard.

ELECTRONIC RESIDENCY APPLICATION SERVICE (ERAS)

In 1995, the AAMC introduced ERAS to applicants in obstetrics and gynecology. ERAS allows your Dean's office to transmit your applications to residency programs via the Internet. With ERAS it is theoretically much easier to keep track of all the documents and forms in your application: you will know exactly what went to whom. After its pilot in 1995–96, ERAS will be expanded to other specialties, with full implementation to most specialties covered in the NRMP Match expected in the next few years.

With ERAS, you fill out a uniform application on a Windows PC computer (Sorry, no Mac version yet). An ERAS student packet includes a "Student Workstation" diskette, a "Student Data" diskette, as well as instruction material. You can install the software on a home computer; however, some schools are also setting up computer stations expressly for ERAS users. ERAS can also be installed on a library network; check with your student affairs office.

The intuitive and user-friendly student software automatically guides you through a series of windows to create a personal application diskette (Table 5–7). It's so easy that many students don't even touch the instruction manual. ERAS applications can be customized in two important ways: (1) You can individualize your personal statement for each program; and (2) you can decide which letters of recommendation go to which program, if you have a choice of letters.

After you have completed your "Student Data" diskette, deliver it to your Dean's office. If you are a U.S. medical graduate, the Dean's office of your medical alma mater will process your application disk. ECFMG serves as the dean's office for IMGs and charges a fee for processing. Your photo is then scanned and attached to the application as a means of identification. Unlike the regular application process, however, the program does not have access to your photo until they schedule you for an interview. Your medical school attaches the dean's letter, transcript, and letters of recommendation. The application is then transmitted to selected programs via the Internet. Programs without Internet access receive hard copies of applications. The programs have the option of asking the applicant to complete a secondary application to be mailed directly to the program. If your application is processed by the Dean's office, you can transmit your application at no charge to as many as 10 programs. The ECFMG processing fee also includes up to 10 applications at no additional charge. You are charged for applications above that number on an escalating fee scale.

Except for a handful of minor glitches, ERAS works well. As with any new system, there will be adjustments and corrections to get residual bugs out of the system. Expect a bit of confusion and uncertainty as residency programs make the transition to ERAS. At present, not all programs will accept

ERAS LETS YOU CUSTOMIZE PERSONAL STATEMENTS AND LISTS OF REFERENCES FOR DIFFERENT PROGRAMS.

MAKE SURE YOUR SCHOOL TRANSMITS YOUR ERAS APPLICATION IN A TIMELY MANNER.

DO NOT LET APPLICATION FEES DISCOURAGE YOU FROM SUBMITTING A COMFORTABLE NUMBER OF APPLICATIONS.

TABLE 5-7. Major steps in ERAS.
Fill out common application form
Create a personal statement
Request letters of recommendation
Select programs to receive application

ERAS applications. If the application instructions you receive from a program are not absolutely clear, call the program for the scoop. Stay in touch with your Dean's office for updates on ERAS, including the specialties currently covered.

REFERENCES

Greenburg A et al: Letters of recommendation for surgical residencies: What they say and what they mean. *J Surg Res* 1994;56:192.

Hunt DD et al: Characteristics of dean's letters in 1981 and 1992. *Acad Med* 1993;68;905.

Leiden LI, Miller GD: National survey of writers of dean's letters for residency applications. *J Med Educ* 1986;61:943.

Vanderbilt School of Medicine Guide to Residency Applications. Vanderbilt University, 1994.

Wagoner NE et al: Factors used by program directors to select residents. *J Med Educ* 1986;61:12.

Zagumny MJ, Rudolph J: Comparing medical students' and residency directors' ratings of criteria used to select residents. *Acad Med* 1992;67:613.

The Curriculum Vitae

In the world of applications and interviews, the CV or the resumé is the equivalent of the 1-minute bullet patient presentation. It should be concise yet complete. A well-written CV places a succinct, factual yet positive account of your academic, career, and extracurricular accomplishments at the fingertips of the residency director. The CV works with the rest of your application to win you an interview. After that, the rest is up to you. You should create a preliminary CV early in the process (ie, during May–July) so that your letter writers can use it as a reference source. You will also want it close to hand as you work on your personal statement. You can fine-tune and expand your CV at the end of the summer.

WHAT'S IN A CV?

A CV typically can include the following elements:

- **Name and address:** Stick with the same name that you use in your applications, dean's letter, transcripts, and correspondence with the programs and the matching service. Make sure you include an address and a phone number where program directors can reach you during the entire interview season. Give a secondary address and phone number (ie, parents') if no one is at your primary address when you are away during the interviewing season.

- **Objective:** A terse, 1-sentence statement of your residency and career goals. Include only if your career goals are not readily apparent to the residency director (eg, a fellowship and academic practice in hand surgery after a residency in orthopedic surgery).

- **Education:** List all major or medically related educational experiences from the present through college. Dual graduate degrees (eg, MD/PhD, MD/MPH, MD/JD) are particularly impressive and should be highlighted. Include the name and place of the institution, your area of study, dates of enrollment, type of degree received, and honors bestowed at graduation (eg, graduating cum laude). If you are a U.S. senior medical student, list your expected graduation date.

TABLE 6-1. Information not appropriate in a CV.

► **Honors:** Include any awards and scholarships that you have received during your med school years, as well as the most important awards and scholarships from your undergraduate years. If you did well in school or on the boards, list your honors and board scores.

► **Publications:** Catalog any abstracts and papers published, in press, or submitted for publication. Format each publication as a detailed bibliographic reference. Also list research presented or talks given at conferences/poster sessions.

► **Extracurricular activities:** Include the most important long-term activities you were involved in during medical school or recently, if you have already graduated. This category would include such things as community service projects, committee work, participation in student organizations, etc.

► **Work experience:** List all major or medically related work experiences, whether paid or volunteer (eg, paramedic work, nursing). Include dates of work experience.

► **Personal:** List hobbies and interests that define you. Also mention any special qualifications or skills that might enhance your effectiveness as a house officer (eg, foreign language training, knowledge of sign language for the deaf, computer skills, etc.).

The phrase "references available upon request" seen in most non-medical CVs is redundant, since letters of recommendation are a required element of the application. Sometimes it helps to list your references by name in the CV, especially if they are particularly illustrious and widely respected.

Note that certain information is **not** appropriate for a medical professional CV (Table 6–1). You may have to consider including information about citizenship or visa status if you are an IMG.

HOW DO I PUT TOGETHER MY CV?

Study the sample CVs starting on page 89 to get a feel for the appearance you want in your finished CV. On a word processor, fill in information under the categories listed above. If you have nothing to say under a category, do not include it. Note that most CVs will start with "Name/Address" and "Education" and end with "Personal." In the middle, however, you can rearrange the order of the remaining categories to emphasize strengths and downplay less impressive areas. Refer to the sample CVs to see various designs available.

After inputting the basic information, edit your document into a professional and attractive format and style using the sample CVs as a guide. See Table 6–2 for specific writing tips. Since your CV will be read during the high-volume screening process, give the screeners a break. Make sure that your CV is pleasing to the eye (Table 6–3). Keep your language terse; sentence fragments often suffice. Use vivid nouns and active verbs (Tables 6–4, 6–5) to demonstrate strength, enthusiasm, and initiative. Pay **very** careful attention to style and punctuation. While no one expects medical students to take graduate seminars in English grammar and syntax, blunders in these areas won't help your application. Medicine is a detail oriented specialty, and sloppiness can be interpreted as evidence of carelessness or lack of motivation. If you have any further doubts, refer to the sample CVs, show your draft

ARRANGE THE ELEMENTS OF YOUR CV TO HIGHLIGHT YOUR STRONG POINTS.

TABLE 6-2. CV writing tips.

- Organize categories to highlight strengths.
- If you're an older applicant, try to avoid unexplained gaps in timeline.
- Use terse, precise, and vivid language.
- Create parallel structure in lists (eg, each item in a list starts with a verb).
- Follow consistent punctuation rules.
- Follow consistent capitalization rules.
- When in doubt, consult a style manual or a professional editor.

to a friend with good writing skills, or consult a manual of style such as Strunk and White's *Elements of Style*.

Ask your career adviser and at least one other person to read the CV and provide feedback on the following: appearance/legibility, ease of reading, grammar, punctuation, and style (Table 6–3). After making any necessary revisions, make copies from a laser printer onto high-quality paper. Choose a heavy cotton bond paper in white or a neutral color to make your CV stand out in a pile (Table 6–6). Alternatively, you can make a master copy and take it to a copy center, choose your paper (most of these places have a good selection of appropriate colors and bond weights), and make high-quality photocopies on the spot.

If you don't have access to a computer or laser printer, don't know how to use one, or just freeze when it comes to putting your life history on paper, you can always have your CV created and reproduced by a copy center (eg, Kinko's) or by a resume specialist as listed in the Yellow Pages. It's true that an overworked secretary in the student affairs office may assist you or do the job for free, but professional service is usually more effective and efficient.

AVOID THE COLORS OF A RAINBOW.

KISSES OF DEATH

Lastly, we are providing you with a handy checklist of no-nos for CVs. Any one of these can be a killer. To repeat advice given earlier, have your adviser and another competent person read your CV, with particular attention to the following:

TABLE 6-3. CV layout and design tips.

- Allow for generous margins (1–1.5 inches).
- Limit resumé to 2 pages.
- Avoid splitting a section when going from page 1 to page 2.
- Try a serif font as the base text font for better legibility. Save sans serif for section headers.
- Do not go below 12 points for font size and 14 points for leading.
- Stay true to your fonts. Too many is distracting and gaudy.
- Be consistent with section headers in style and formatting.
- Boldface your name in any publications cited.
- Use boldface, small caps, italics, and bullet symbols sparingly. Avoid underlining.
- Print CV on a laser printer.
- Print CV on a heavyweight, cotton bond paper. Use a neutral color (eg, ivory).
- Make sure the finished CV photocopies well.

TABLE 6-4. Action verbs.

accelerated	directed	lectured	reorganized
accomplished	effected	led	revamped
achieved	elucidated	maintained	reviewed
adapted	established	managed	revised
administered	evaluated	mastered	scheduled
analyzed	examined	motivated	set up
approved	expanded	operated	solved
attained	expedited	organized	streamlined
clarified	facilitated	originated	structured
completed	found	participated	studied
conceived	generated	performed	supervised
conducted	improved	pinpointed	supported
controlled	increased	planned	synthesized
coordinated	influenced	proposed	taught
created	implemented	proved	trained
delegated	initiated	provided	translated
demonstrated	instructed	recommended	used
designed	interpreted	reduced	won
developed	launched	reinforced	wrote

▶ **Unprofessional appearance.** Do **not** write your CV by hand or use a typewriter. Dot matrix is also dead. Laser printing at 300 dpi is now the standard; 600 dpi laser output, also readily available, is slightly better. If you find a mistake on the CV, no matter how minor, print out a new, corrected version. Do **not** make corrections, handwritten or typed, on the CV. Use only high-quality, heavyweight bond paper.

▶ **Inaccuracies or exaggerations.** Present your talents and accomplishments in the best light possible, but do not misrepresent them. Residency directors have many ways of verifying your claims. Even a minor "misrepresentation" can have a major impact on your credibility.

▶ **Too lengthy.** Do not exceed two pages in length unless you have really stellar experience and an impressive list of publications to justify more space. Remember that this is a capsule summary of your career to date, not an extended autobiography.

▶ **Misspellings, poor grammar.** These unspectacular mistakes will only contribute to an image of carelessness or incompetence, particularly since most word processors make it easy to check spelling and grammar.

▶ **Weak writing.** Verbosity kills; keep your sentences short and succinct. Specifics count; the more precisely you can describe your experience, the better the reader can picture—and appreciate—what you say. Stay away from bland nouns and passive verbs.

TABLE 6-6. Appropriate colors and patterns for CV paper.

White
Ivory
Beige
Light gray
Flannel pattern
Speckle pattern

TABLE 6-5. Concrete nouns and positive modifiers.

ability	competent	proficient	technical
actively	consistent	qualified	unique
capacity	effectively	resourceful	versatile
competence	pertinent	substantially	vigorous

SAMPLE CVs

FIGURE 6-1A

This applicant has a well-rounded CV with no real outstanding achievements. But because he is applying to several academic training programs, he chooses to list his research experience first.

WILLIAM BRADFORD THOMAS
325 Drummond Lane
Louisville, KY 40322
(512) 555-7457

EDUCATION

1991-Present **University of Louisville School of Medicine.**
M.D. anticipated May 1995.

1987-1991 **Centre College of Kentucky.**
B.S., Biology and Psychology, *magna cum laude*.

RESEARCH

Summer, 1992 **Summer Research Fellow.**
Stefan Maguire, PhD, Hormone Research Institute. Elucidated the role of glutamic acid decarboxylase in the autoimmune pathogenesis of insulin dependent diabetes mellitus.

> Do not forget to list your principal investigator

Summer, 1990 **Research Assistant.**
Richard Woodbridge, MD, University of Kentucky Medical Research Building. Analyzed flow characteristics of IV infusion pumps to evaluate their accuracy in removing outflow of spent dialysate and ultrafiltrate.

PUBLICATIONS

W. Thomas and S. Maguire. "Is GAD_{65} localized to synaptic-like vesicles in ß-pancreatic cells?" 1992 School of Medicine Research Poster Session.

> Text is indented to keep clean, vertical look

R. Woodbridge, **W. Thomas,** D. Arnold, J. Funk. "Accuracy of IV Pumps in CAVHD." *American Society for Artificial Internal Organs: 1991 Abstracts,* 1991, p. 78.

HONORS & AWARDS

1991 **Michael Ryan Biology Prize.** Centre College.

1991 **Jeffrey Scott McBride Leadership Award.** Centre College.

1990 **Phi Beta Kappa**

1987-1991 **Trustee Scholarship.** Half tuition merit scholarship.

Sample CV No. 1

FIGURE 6-1B

WILLIAM BRADFORD THOMAS

EXTRACURRICULAR

1994-Present **Faculty Student Network Committee.** Organized events and meetings for faculty advisers and medical students.

School of Medicine Representative, Registration Fee Committee. Committee allocates student fees to student organizations and services.

1992-1993 **Peer Counselor, Campus Health.** Provided counseling and support for first-year medical students.

1991-Present **Homeless Health Clinic.** Evaluated and treated homeless patients as medical volunteer in homeless shelter.

1991-1992 **Vice-president, AMA–Medical Student Section Chapter.** Organized health fairs and guest speakers for medical school chapter.

PROFESSIONAL MEMBERSHIPS

1991-Present **American Medical Association, Medical Student Section**

1994-Present **American Academy of Pediatrics, Medical Student Section**

PERSONAL

Proficient in American sign language.
Hobbies include volleyball, jogging.

Use "action" verbs to give an active tone

FIGURE 6-2A

This CV emphasizes the applicant's considerable research accomplishments. If she were applying to mostly clinical programs, she might alternatively choose to highlight her strong extracurricular activities.

Sarah Lin

Permanent Address	*School Address*
P.O. Box 271 MDSC	234 Melrose Place
Clarksville, IN 47160	Nashville, TN 37215
(812) 555-3952	(619) 555-5456

EDUCATION

Vanderbilt University School of Medicine   *1992 to Present*
Nashville, TN
    MD EXPECTED IN MAY 1996

St. Louis University   *1988 to 1992*
St. Louis, MO
    BA, BIOLOGY AND PSYCHOLOGY, MAGNA CUM LAUDE

RESEARCH

Research Assistant   *Summer, 1993*   ◄────────
University of California, San Diego
    SAMUEL STOCKTON, MD, PHD. Developed a rat model to study the
    inflammatory process in asthma.

Research Assistant   *January, 1993 to May, 1993*
Vanderbilt University School of Medicine
    SHELLEY PISA, MD. Characterized the interactions between anesthetic drugs
    and the erythrocyte Band 3 anion exchange channel.

Research Assistant   *January, 1991 to May, 1992*
St. Louis University
    ANTHONY HILL, PHD. Explored the medicinal value of the plant *Rhamnacea*
    used by South American Indians in wound healing.

Research Assistant   *September, 1991 to December, 1992*
St. Louis University
    TIMOTHY ROBERTS, PHD. Developed protocols for the use of mutant
    strains of *Chlamydomonas* in transformation experiments.

> Alternative way to keep
> dates separated from text

Sample CV No. 2

FIGURE 6-2B

Sarah Lin   2

Include a header if your CV has 2 pages

PUBLICATIONS

C. Anand, V. Beck, T. Carusi, **S. Lin,** contributing author. *Solutions Guide and Study Manual to Retired and Self-Test Questions,* Ashland, OH: Butterfield, 1995.

S. Lin, A. Hill. "Wound healing properties of the *Rhamnacea* plant." *American Journal of Herbal Medicine,* June 1993, Vol. 22, No. 6, pp. 210-212.

EXTRACURRICULAR

St. Thomas Catholic Charity Services   *1994 to Present*
Taught English to Vietnamese refugees and served as interpreter for social workers.

A Room in the Inn   *1993 to Present*
Prepared and served meals in a homeless soup kitchen.

Morari School Project   *1992 to 1993*
Organized health science presentations for elementary school children.

Asian American Medical Student Association   *1992 to Present*
Promoted community and school awareness of health care and Asian culture.

St. Louis University Student Admissions Committee   *1990 to 1992*
Recruited prospective students and aided in the selection process.

Cultural Celebration Committee   *1989 to 1992*
Helped organize an annual undergraduate cultural fair.

PERSONAL

Fluent in Cantonese.
Hobbies include ethnic cuisine and gardening.

Be ready to discuss anything on your CV in detail

FIGURE 6-3A

This applicant has an impressive number of awards and honors. Because she is entering family practice, she emphasizes her community service experience and lists her research on the second page.

Jacquelyn H. Lemmon

School Address
576 London Road, Apt. #5
Tucson, AZ 85719
(602) 555-7456

Permanent Address
2145 Red Valley Drive
Danville, TN 34205
(615) 555-5760

Education

1992–1996   UNIVERSITY OF ARIZONA SCHOOL OF MEDICINE
M.D. expected in May, 1996

1988–1992   WASHINGTON UNIVERSITY
B.S. in Engineering & Policy

Honors & Awards

1994   BRISTOL-MYERS SQUIBB SCHOLAR ◄ - - - - - - - - - - - -

1993–1996   MICROBES AND DEFENSE SOCIETY

1993   DIABETES SUMMER RESEARCH GRANT
Awarded by Diabetes Research and Training Center.

1993   SUMMER RESEARCH GRANT
Awarded by American Society for Lasers in Medicine and Surgery.

1992–1996   JUSTIN POTTER SCHOLARSHIP
Merit award based on leadership potential.

1991–1992   MORTAR BOARD HONOR SOCIETY

1988–1992   JOHN B. ERVIN SCHOLARSHIP

Extracurricular

1992–Present   STUDENT NATIONAL MEDICAL ASSOCIATION
Promoted health care and minority issues. Served as co-chairperson and treasurer of Arizona chapter.

1994–Present   TUCSON CARES
Made lecture presentations on HIV/AIDS to the general public on behalf of agency, which serves HIV/AIDS population.

> All-caps is an alternative to boldfaced text.

Sample CV No. 3.

FIGURE 6-3B

Jacquelyn H. Lemmon

Extracurricular, continued

1992–Present   VARIOUS SERVICE ACTIVITIES
Participated in several community service activities including Inn for the Homeless, Habitat for Humanity, wheelchair ramp construction, role model activities for black youth.

1992   SUBSTANCE ABUSE AND PREVENTION PROGRAM
Counseled high-risk youth as part of a first-year elective.

Research

March–August, 1995   RESEARCH ELECTIVE, CENTERS FOR DISEASE CONTROL AND PREVENTION
Preceptor Richard Woodbridge, MD. Designed methods for collecting and organizing for international importations data. Collected and analyzed 1995 data with comparison to data collected from 1986 to 1994.

1994   RESEARCH ASSISTANT
Preceptor George Sherman, MD. Characterized lymphocytic migration in RSV-infected mice. Results presented at National Medical Fellowships Research Seminar in February, 1995.

Summer, 1993   SUMMER RESEARCH FELLOW
Preceptor Lou Ritter, MD. Tested various pulse structures of the electron laser to evaluate its efficacy in bone ablation.

Summer, 1993   RESEARCH ASSISTANT
Preceptor Lou Ritter, MD. Developed optimal laser firing patterns to achieve minimal thermal buildup in a collagen-based target. Results presented to the Arizona Diabetes Research Training Center.

Personal

Hobbies include jogging, piano, swimming.

2

A good way to present multiple small activities.

FIGURE 6-4

Both a 1-page CV and a 2-page CV are acceptable. Because everything is on 1 page, the order of categories is not as important.

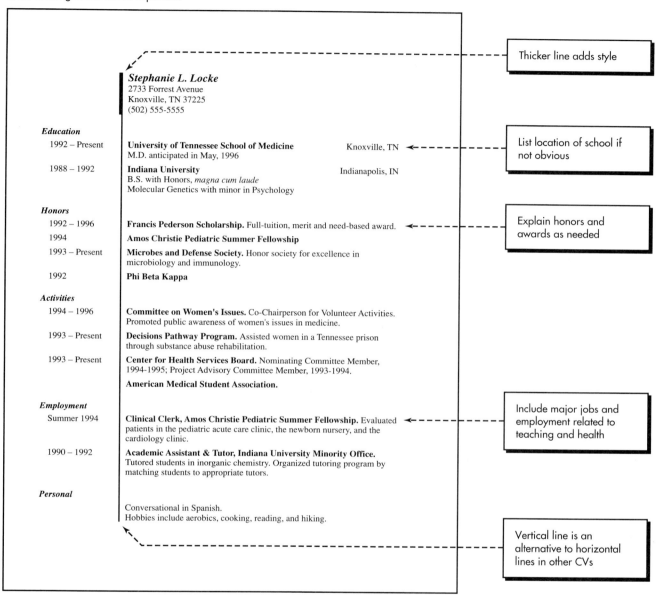

Thicker line adds style

Stephanie L. Locke
2733 Forrest Avenue
Knoxville, TN 37225
(502) 555-5555

Education

1992 – Present **University of Tennessee School of Medicine**   Knoxville, TN
M.D. anticipated in May, 1996

List location of school if not obvious

1988 – 1992 **Indiana University**   Indianapolis, IN
B.S. with Honors, *magna cum laude*
Molecular Genetics with minor in Psychology

Honors

1992 – 1996 **Francis Pederson Scholarship.** Full-tuition, merit and need-based award.

Explain honors and awards as needed

1994 **Amos Christie Pediatric Summer Fellowship**

1993 – Present **Microbes and Defense Society.** Honor society for excellence in microbiology and immunology.

1992 **Phi Beta Kappa**

Activities

1994 – 1996 **Committee on Women's Issues.** Co-Chairperson for Volunteer Activities. Promoted public awareness of women's issues in medicine.

1993 – Present **Decisions Pathway Program.** Assisted women in a Tennessee prison through substance abuse rehabilitation.

1993 – Present **Center for Health Services Board.** Nominating Committee Member, 1994-1995; Project Advisory Committee Member, 1993-1994.

American Medical Student Association.

Employment

Summer 1994 **Clinical Clerk, Amos Christie Pediatric Summer Fellowship.** Evaluated patients in the pediatric acute care clinic, the newborn nursery, and the cardiology clinic.

Include major jobs and employment related to teaching and health

1990 – 1992 **Academic Assistant & Tutor, Indiana University Minority Office.** Tutored students in inorganic chemistry. Organized tutoring program by matching students to appropriate tutors.

Personal

Conversational in Spanish.
Hobbies include aerobics, cooking, reading, and hiking.

Vertical line is an alternative to horizontal lines in other CVs

Sample CV No. 4.

REFERENCES

"Resume Guidelines." Southworth Paper Company, 1995.

The Personal Statement

Writing the personal statement can be excruciating. It's hard to start and harder yet to know exactly what the selection committee wants to read. A draft that feels inspired at the moment of composition often seems hokey 2 days later. As much as you might like to, you can't simply rehash your AMCAS personal statement, as it usually does not address the same issues covered by a good personal statement for the Match (ie, the traits of a good medical student are often different from those of a good house officer). In addition, despite all the trouble you take to write it, the personal statement is often seen by residency selection committees as an opportunity to weed out applicants. Thus, while an outstanding personal statement might salvage a mediocre application, a bad one can cripple a strong application.

Most selection committees tend to underanalyze (or ignore) personal statements during the high-volume screening process, and to over-scrutinize them during the knock-down, drag-out ranking sessions that follow the screening. It is common to see otherwise well-qualified applicants slide 20 to 40 positions on a rank list at the last minute because the selection committee suddenly perceived something in their personal statements as negative.

For this reason, do not take the personal statement lightly. It is the one part of the application over which you have **total** control, and your one chance for creative expression. Residency directors often use the personal statement to check for qualities not readily apparent from your application form—such as maturity, enthusiasm, thoughtfulness, humility, stability, and a willingness to learn. Note the characteristics that directors look for in future house officers; if your personal statement conveys these qualities, it will strengthen your application.

PICKING THE TOPICS

The strain of writing a personal statement begins with brainstorming—trying to figure out which topics to cover. All personal statements, however, are similar at their core. All are "revelation stories" to some degree—showing how your upbringing, life events, and intellectual interests have influenced your current specialty and career aspirations. Most residency directors want

A GREAT PERSONAL STATEMENT MIGHT HELP AN APPLICATION, BUT A BAD ONE WILL KILL IT.

THE FOUR A'S OF A SUCCESSFUL HOUSE OFFICER: (1) ATTITUDE; (2) AFFABILITY; (3) AVAILABILITY; (4) ABILITY.

to understand an applicant's personal reasons for seeking to enter the specialty, as well as his or her professional goals.

We've taken the liberty of listing questions you should ask yourself when building your statement. Thoughtful answers to 2 or 3 of these questions should give you enough substance for a good first draft. The safest and most familiar topics include: (1) reasons for choosing a specialty; (2) career plans; (3) accomplishments; and (4) interests outside medicine. Note that each of these topics implies a different time frame and has its own tense (past, present, future, conditional, etc.). It is up to you to decide how much backtracking, present-day analysis, and future-gazing you would like to do.

(1) **What are my reasons for choosing the specialty?** Most committee members who will review your application are curious about your reasons for choosing their specialty. Most applicants discuss the nature of the work, the patient population, the intellectual challenges, or the desire to make a unique contribution to medicine. Mentioning financial and lifestyle reasons, though they may have played a part in your decision-making process, is a faux pas in a personal statement.

(2) **What are my career plans?** The overused party line is to talk in vague generalities about having a clinical practice with possibly some academic involvement. Be as specific as possible without antagonizing anyone who might be reading your statement. Think about discussing the fit between your career goals on the one hand and your disposition and personal goals on the other. An ability to articulate clear and realistic plans will give the reader the sense that you have a firm understanding of their specialty.

(3) **What accomplishments do I want to emphasize?** You can use part of your personal statement to highlight a noteworthy activity or achievement that might have otherwise escaped the notice of the selection committee. You can skim through your CV and Dean's letter to pinpoint such achievements. Use them to demonstrate your desire to enter the specialty, reveal a positive personal quality, or illustrate your worthiness to enter the field. Avoid, however, the temptation to rehash your CV in your personal statement.

(4) **What outside interests do I have?** Selection committees need to be assured that, apart from working 100+-hour weeks during the tougher rotations, depriving yourself of sleep and exercise on a regular basis, and actually paying a medical school to do this, you are otherwise a semi-normal person. Touch on extracurricular interests to add depth to the presentation of your character, or to illustrate personal qualities (eg, participation in community activities indicates both a sense of responsibility and a capacity for active involvement).

(5) **What contributions can I make to the specialty and the residency program?** Hold forth about your love of teaching, years of leadership training, computer expertise, and rich parents eager to donate big bucks to the program (just kidding). As discussed above, these considerations can be brought out in the context of accomplishments, reasons for entering the specialty, or outside interests.

STAY AWAY FROM FINANCIAL AND LIFESTYLE REASONS IN A PERSONAL STATEMENT.

DO NOT REHASH YOUR CV IN THE PERSONAL STATEMENT.

DAMAGE CONTROL

In addition, you can carefully use a personal statement to address one or more of the following concerns:

How can I compensate for serious problems or weaknesses in my application? If you recognize that your record contains a real blot, you may preempt the selection committee's concern. Here is a chance to defend your record and demonstrate your ability to learn from poor performances and negative incidents. However, be careful not to (1) sound defensive, or (2) dwell on the negative. Discussion of negatives can easily backfire, especially by drawing attention to something that might have otherwise passed unnoticed. Find yourself a trusted adviser to discuss both general strategy and the wording of the statement itself.

Are there any remaining issues (outstanding problems) that I would like to discuss during an interview? If you believe that you cannot adequately address certain concerns in a personal statement, you may choose to indicate that you would be more than happy to discuss them during the interview. Again, review this option with your adviser.

PERSONAL STATEMENT TIPS

1. **Know your audience.** Understand what your target programs want to see and what you have to offer in return. Then, choose 1 or 2 topics from the preceding list, in addition to reasons for entering the specialty and future career plans, to anchor your personal statement. The prototypical statement has 4 to 6 paragraphs (Figure 7–1).

FIGURE 7-1

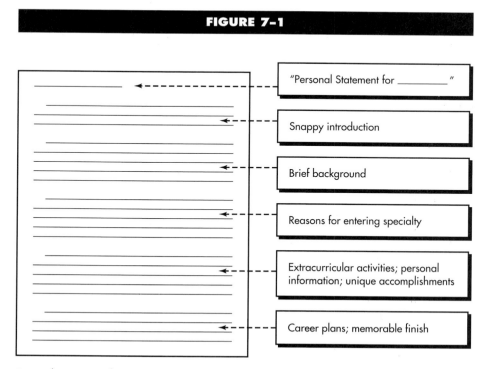

Personal statement schematic.

2. **Be straightforward in your writing.** It's perfectly safe and actually desirable. As in your CV, stick with active verbs; avoid passive sentence structures. Writing manifests personality; you want to come across as energetic and ready for action.

3. **Vary your wording and sentence structure with the help of a thesaurus.** Most good word processors have an on-line thesaurus. Spell out non-standard abbreviations and explain local jargon; otherwise avoid them.

4. **Edit and proofread your work carefully.** Use the spell-checker in your word processor, then read the statement word for word for misspellings, since a word processor cannot spell-check in context. Grammar checkers give mixed results but usually do no harm. A professional editor can be cheap ($10 to $25 per hour) and preferable, if you can find a good one.

5. **Don't crowd your page with too much text.** Allow generous page margins (1 to 1.5 inches) and adequate spacing between each line (a minimum leading of 13 to 14 points, for you word processor geeks). Don't forget to indent paragraphs and add at least a half line between each paragraph.

6. **Choose an appropriate font.** Stick to serif fonts (eg, Times Roman, Garamond). Sans serif fonts (eg, Helvetica, Arial) are more difficult to read and photocopy poorly.

7. **Get a second opinion.** Have your statement read at least by your adviser and a second person with writing and editing skills.

8. **Revise—to a reasonable extent.**

9. **Don't get lost in the shuffle.** If your personal statement is separate from your application, then put your name and your NRMP identification number on top of the statement.

10. **Don't skimp on printing.** Print the final copies on a laser printer. If the personal statement is separate from the application, print it on the same paper you used for your CV.

KISSES OF DEATH FOR A PERSONAL STATEMENT

Since the personal statement is your big opportunity to impress committee members with a winning combination of skills and talents, it's tempting to indulge in ruffles and flourishes of one kind or another. Every year students strive for ways to jazz up their statements. Unfortunately, most of them end up falling into one of the following traps:

Self-congratulatory statements: If you happen to be God's gift to medicine, it is much better to let other people say that for you in your letters of recommendation and the Dean's letter. Your personal statement should radiate confidence and a sense of self-worth without straying into arrogance.

Self-centered statements: Don't let the reader drown in a sea of "I"s. Overuse of the first person singular can be interpreted either as a sign of self-centeredness or as a lack of writing skill.

Emotional stories: Heart-tugging stories about personal experiences with patients, personal illness, or an illness in the family that illustrate your motivations, your understanding of medicine, or your professional/personal qualities can have a spectacular effect. Unless you're Michael Crichton, however (who never finished a residency anyway), writing medical melo-

A STATEMENT SHOULD RADIATE CONFIDENCE AND SELF-WORTH, NOT ARROGANCE.

drama carries the risk of the reader's not "buying" your experience. This is especially true if you assign too much emotional value or influence to a specific experience (eg, inflated humanism). Will the average program director really believe that one experience with a patient revolutionized your outlook on medicine, let alone your whole philosophy of life?

If you do include a personal account, describe it in rich detail and bring it to a satisfactory conclusion. Residency directors may be annoyed by influential life experiences that are described in a trite, superficial or incomplete manner.

Overgeneralizations: Unsupported claims that you are hardworking, efficient, curious, etc. may ring hollow without specific examples to back them up. Let your accomplishments, activities, and patient experiences attest to your professional and personal traits. Make sure your letter writers have a copy of your personal statement so they can corroborate your strengths.

Use of tired analogies: Avoid trite metaphors, such as comparing medical school to a box of chocolates. Other overworked cliches include "life is a road/path," "life is a journey," and "life is a book." If you think you have a genuinely creative idea, have several reviewers read your draft for honest feedback.

Gimmicky writing: Sometimes students try to impress readers with their creative writing skills. For example, one applicant wrote his statement in the form of an admit note. Attempts at literary originality may lead to speculation about the existence of significant psychopathology rather than to an appreciation of the writer's uniqueness. But all this doesn't mean you have to be boring. A conventional statement can still project enthusiasm, vitality, and wit. Committees are by nature conservative.

Inconsistencies: Your statement should agree with the rest of your application. If your transcripts show you to be an average student, don't write about yourself as the next Einstein. Your statement should also jibe with itself. If you want to be a rural family practitioner, what evidence can you present to demonstrate your interest in rural health care?

Long statements: Unless you're going into psychiatry, limit your personal statement to 1 page. Residency directors who read hundreds of essays view 2-page statements as divine retribution for their past sins. If you're afraid you won't be able to fit all your topics within the limit, ask your adviser or a friend to check your writing style for conciseness; it may be that critical editing is all you need.

Digressions: Every sentence you write should count; it should be clear in purpose and content. There is no need or room to repeat yourself if you made your point the first time.

Illegible statements: Personal statements that have a crammed appearance or are otherwise hard to read will only trigger migraines in your readers. Review the previous section on proofreading and printing for specific pointers about your statement's visual appearance.

Misspellings, poor grammar: Although this seems to be an obvious pitfall, people stumble into it more often than you would expect. Don't weaken an otherwise good statement with typos or mistakes in usage. Run your statement through the spelling checker if you have a word processor, and ask at least 2 people (including your adviser) to proofread and critique your essay.

SAVE THE BOWL OF CHERRIES.

LONG STATEMENTS GET PENALIZED—NOT FAIR, BUT THAT'S LIFE.

WRITE, REWRITE, EDIT AND PROOFREAD.

SAMPLE EXCERPTS

We have included excerpts from actual personal statements as examples of do's and don'ts for certain issues. Names and locations have been changed to protect the writers' identities, but otherwise you're reading what the residency directors read. Most of the applicants behind these statements matched at top-flight institutions across the country. The comments which accompany our examples are derived from the observations of several residency directors, admissions committee members, and a professional editor. We hope that the critiques will help you acquire a "feel" for good form as well as good content. Keep in mind, however, that no two residency directors (even in the same specialty) read a personal statement with the same opinions and preferences.

Strong or Engaging Openings

Example #1. This applicant in emergency medicine draws on rich family and cultural traditions and values. A residency director reading this introduction is not only making the acquaintance of an applicant, they are learning about the applicant's entire value system.

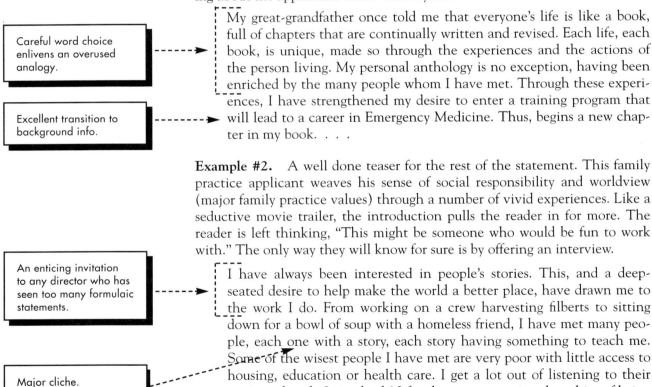

Careful word choice enlivens an overused analogy.

> My great-grandfather once told me that everyone's life is like a book, full of chapters that are continually written and revised. Each life, each book, is unique, made so through the experiences and the actions of the person living. My personal anthology is no exception, having been enriched by the many people whom I have met. Through these experiences, I have strengthened my desire to enter a training program that will lead to a career in Emergency Medicine. Thus, begins a new chapter in my book. . . .

Excellent transition to background info.

Example #2. A well done teaser for the rest of the statement. This family practice applicant weaves his sense of social responsibility and worldview (major family practice values) through a number of vivid experiences. Like a seductive movie trailer, the introduction pulls the reader in for more. The reader is left thinking, "This might be someone who would be fun to work with." The only way they will know for sure is by offering an interview.

An enticing invitation to any director who has seen too many formulaic statements.

Major cliche.

A noble reason to become a doctor. But why medicine versus other altruistic vocations?

> I have always been interested in people's stories. This, and a deep-seated desire to help make the world a better place, have drawn me to the work I do. From working on a crew harvesting filberts to sitting down for a bowl of soup with a homeless friend, I have met many people, each one with a story, each story having something to teach me. Some of the wisest people I have met are very poor with little access to housing, education or health care. I get a lot out of listening to their stories; what do I give back? I first began to question the ethics of being a responsible listener when I went to Nicaragua as a Spanish interpreter. I was with a group of agronomists on a struggling agricultural cooperative nestled deep in the mountains of Matagalpa. The life was hard, but the work was fascinating and the setting beautiful. I finally got up the courage to ask the cooperative leader if I could stay longer. He smiled, "You gringos eat a lot. Now, maybe if you were a doctor. . . ." I chose to become a physician as a way to work intimately with people and hear their stories. But, just as importantly, it is a way to tangibly improve their lives.

Example #3.   This applicant in anesthesiology successfully recycles a familiar travel theme with vivid imagery. The opening paragraph introduces a traveler enriched by his adventures. Unfortunately, we begin to sense that his actions have an unsettled, random quality.

While driving in the Mojave Desert, I turned off Highway 14 onto a dirt path. The road was crisscrossed by many other trails. Small hills blocked my view of what lay ahead on each road. Unable to see what each road led to, I randomly chose to drive along one road, then another, and then another. Every new direction possessed its own beauty and worth. One road revealed towering, sand-carved cliffs with striated bands of crimson, orange, and tan spotted with turquoise. Another road led to a lone Joshua tree standing majestically in the desert grass. Each new path inspired a new thought. I have had a similar experience in medicine.

> One hopes his choice of specialty was more deliberate. Rewrite to show some method to this madness.

> Vivid! You feel like you're there.

> Weak tie-in to medicine.

Example #4.   This applicant in orthopedic surgery wants to return to the Midwest after training at an East Coast medical school. He combines the family legacy of an immigrant background with the rustic, traditional values of Middle America. However, by playing up the Midwest, he runs the risk of turning off East and West Coast directors in a highly competitive specialty in which applicants often have to apply coast-to-coast to match.

Growing up in the small farming community of Vernon in east-central Indiana, I have experienced a spectrum of attitudes unique to a rural population. Folks here are down to earth, with simple, relaxed lifestyles. It was here where I have lived almost all my life, moving from Birmingham, Alabama, my birthplace, at 9 months of age. It was here where my father set up his urology practice 30 years ago, having come from abroad with little more than a dream for a successful future. It was here, amidst the cornfields and cattle which I could see from my bedroom window, that I grew up with my older sister and younger brother under a strict, coherent value system of hard work, motivation, dedication, and perseverance.

> Back off a little on the rural imagery here. We get the point.

> Nice way of associating yourself with a set of values. Stating the same directly can come off as presumptuous.

Reasons for Entering Specialty

Example #1.   The following comes close to being a model illustration of good organization and presentation of motivations for pursuing a specialty. The applicant is obviously comfortable discussing the specialty, and appears sincere in his enthusiasm without being patronizing. The writing is sparse, but neither dry nor flat.

I grew up with surgery in my blood, but it was not until the middle of my third year of medical school that I discovered that I wanted to practice orthopedic surgery. It was at this time that I was first exposed to orthopedic surgery at Springfield Memorial Hospital. My love of being in the operating room, combined with the very precise mechanical and technical nature of orthopedic surgery, sparked my interest in the field. Perhaps the feature that fascinates me the most about orthopedics is that it is both a craft and a science. I enjoy the "hands-on" nature of orthopedic surgery, both in clinic and in the operating room. I am also attracted to the diversity of orthopedic cases and the vast amount of di-

> A bit cliche.

> Note the number of concrete reasons why orthopedics appeals to him.

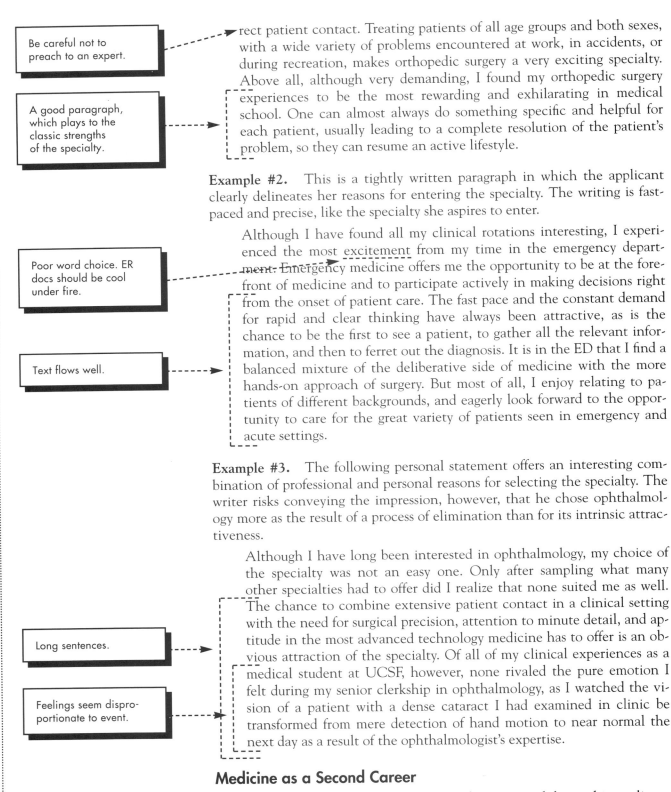

Be careful not to preach to an expert.

rect patient contact. Treating patients of all age groups and both sexes, with a wide variety of problems encountered at work, in accidents, or during recreation, makes orthopedic surgery a very exciting specialty. Above all, although very demanding, I found my orthopedic surgery experiences to be the most rewarding and exhilarating in medical school. One can almost always do something specific and helpful for each patient, usually leading to a complete resolution of the patient's problem, so they can resume an active lifestyle.

A good paragraph, which plays to the classic strengths of the specialty.

Example #2. This is a tightly written paragraph in which the applicant clearly delineates her reasons for entering the specialty. The writing is fast-paced and precise, like the specialty she aspires to enter.

Although I have found all my clinical rotations interesting, I experienced the most excitement from my time in the emergency department. Emergency medicine offers me the opportunity to be at the forefront of medicine and to participate actively in making decisions right from the onset of patient care. The fast pace and the constant demand for rapid and clear thinking have always been attractive, as is the chance to be the first to see a patient, to gather all the relevant information, and then to ferret out the diagnosis. It is in the ED that I find a balanced mixture of the deliberative side of medicine with the more hands-on approach of surgery. But most of all, I enjoy relating to patients of different backgrounds, and eagerly look forward to the opportunity to care for the great variety of patients seen in emergency and acute settings.

Poor word choice. ER docs should be cool under fire.

Text flows well.

Example #3. The following personal statement offers an interesting combination of professional and personal reasons for selecting the specialty. The writer risks conveying the impression, however, that he chose ophthalmology more as the result of a process of elimination than for its intrinsic attractiveness.

Although I have long been interested in ophthalmology, my choice of the specialty was not an easy one. Only after sampling what many other specialties had to offer did I realize that none suited me as well. The chance to combine extensive patient contact in a clinical setting with the need for surgical precision, attention to minute detail, and aptitude in the most advanced technology medicine has to offer is an obvious attraction of the specialty. Of all of my clinical experiences as a medical student at UCSF, however, none rivaled the pure emotion I felt during my senior clerkship in ophthalmology, as I watched the vision of a patient with a dense cataract I had examined in clinic be transformed from mere detection of hand motion to near normal the next day as a result of the ophthalmologist's expertise.

Long sentences.

Feelings seem disproportionate to event.

Medicine as a Second Career

Example #1. In contrast to some second-career candidates, this applicant emphasizes the common ground between pediatrics and his previous career. In fact, the paragraph does not explain why he decided to make the career change.

For 5 years prior to medical school, I taught computer science in grades 2–12 at a private bilingual school. I loved working with children and their families and had the joy of seeing my students learn and grow over a number of years. These same preferences led me to an interest in pediatrics as a specialty. Pediatrics is a heady mixture of the exotic and the mundane, of glowing health and desperate illness. It offers a wide variety of patients, a mix of common and uncommon disorders, a practice based in growth and development, and the possibility to make a real difference in the lives of patients and their families.

> Smooth transition.

> Motherhood and apple pie.

Example #2. Like many second-career applicants, this student also felt something meaningful was missing from his career. However, he makes one misstep. In contrasting his future career in psychiatry with his past work in mathematics, he puts down the latter unnecessarily. It is true that making a career change is not easy, but it may sound overblown to characterize it as a monumental achievement.

My pure math activities were enjoyable for themselves, yet I had a growing sense that community service was what gave my life meaning and direction. Did I want to get to the end of my life and answer "What had I done?" with "I proved theorems"? Hoping to use science to help others rather than merely to create more science, I concluded I might be happiest in the long run in medicine, and courageously decided to change careers. So far, medicine has more than fulfilled my expectations as a context to combine the heart and the head. I am particularly intrigued by the doctor-patient relationship, which impresses me as a seamless blend of problem solving, hypothesis-testing, trust-building, and appreciation of the patients' individuality.

> Don't denigrate previous accomplishments.

Example #3. This is a well-written paragraph that demonstrates remarkable insight and maturity of thought. The first half of the paragraph is a concise description of his activities during the year off. In the latter half, the applicant shares what he has learned without portraying it as an unprecedented revelation.

After my third year of medical school, I pursued my interest in policy issues studying for a Masters Degree in Public Health at Emory. I spent the year exploring the epidemiology of infectious diseases, options for health care reform, and the empowerment of low-income communities. I learned useful skills in biostatistics and qualitative evaluation, and gained a global perspective on our health care system. At times, however, our discussions of abstract ideas and numbers felt too far removed from the realities of people's lives. I became convinced that debates about health care delivery should be rooted in concrete clinical practice, in the stories of patients and providers. My experience in public health taught me that doctors have a special role in society because they are trusted by patients and respected by policy makers. This combination allows physicians to be potent advocates for their patients and their community.

> Good summary.

> Nice tie-in with his interest in family practice. Clear, concise, and thoughtful.

Strong Extracurricular/Community Accomplishments

Example #1. This applicant has an impressive list of extracurricular activities and achievements. But it is the richness of detail that convinces you that she is diversified and involved in her community.

This sentence preempts any concern that the writer's extracurricular activities would interfere with her duties as a resident.

Self-motivated, I work vigorously at my research, teaching and patient care. However, it is also very important to me to continue furthering my personal interests, including the creative preparation and presentation of gourmet foods, wreathmaking, and horse training. Especially rewarding is my weekend volunteer work with the Stony Brook Riding Club for the Handicapped that entails rounding up the herd at 6 AM, feeding, grooming, tacking, and assisting the physically and/or mentally disabled riders in any way necessary. Annual CPR organization and instruction to the public brings important education to the community and keeps me abreast of the laymen's current fund of medical knowledge. Additionally, my family background of being the eldest daughter of an architect and a nuclear medicine technologist from Indonesia has led me to a longtime interest in the integration of drawing and science, namely medical illustration. My aspiration is to obtain formal training in illustration technique when my medical education is complete; in the meantime, I hope to continue publishing my drawings and using them in presentations during my residency.

Be careful not to digress; they need a house officer, not an illustrator.

Example #2. It is not enough to list your academic accomplishments CV-style. This student highlights the significance of his academic activities in clear, well-organized expository writing.

Computer consulting work has provided me with close contact with creative researchers in science and medicine. A 2-year thesis project with Dr. Elizabeth Rutter challenged my skills in relational databases, clinical record-keeping systems and exploratory statistical techniques.

Emphasizes professional skills developed during the project.

In the laboratory of Dr. Jeffrey Greenberg, I applied innovative real-time video microscopy and image processing techniques to fundamental growth and cell-division questions in cell biology. Through my lab work I have developed interests in improving the quality and utility of medical technology for clinical decision-making.

Attempts to connect basic science to clinical research.

I have supplemented medical school by being an active participant in basic biomedical science. In addition to medicine, I am familiar with the tools and vocabulary of modern molecular biology. I read a wide variety of clinical and scientific journals, and use literature searching extensively.

Applicant seeking research oriented residency skillfully weaves in additional academic activities.

Poor Academic Performance and Other Blemishes

Example #1. There is very little room for excuses in medicine. You either got the job done or you didn't. Unless you have a glaring blemish on your record, excuses will only cause the committee to focus on your weaknesses. In this example the applicant tries to explain why he did not snag more honors. If he had kept his mouth shut, few would have considered this to be a major problem.

On the wards, I found it easy to develop rapport with patients and team members. Ward medicine stimulated my love of scientific inquiry and problem solving. I found enthusiasm, dependability, focused presentations and resilience keys to success. I excelled in medicine clerkships, but my other interests have often required making compromises in pursuing honors in all rotations.

> Risky to make excuses.

Personal Experiences

Example #1. In some cases, applicants can use general life experiences to become better practitioners. This student, in a dramatic and somewhat risky fashion, indicates that he is able to learn even from painful experiences.

Unfortunately, not every experience that I had at the University of Rochester was so good, such as the time when I was mugged at gunpoint while walking home from Norton Memorial Hospital on a chilly December evening during my General Surgery rotation. Having been raised in the small town of Brevard, crime was somewhat of a foreign concept to me, as it was just something that I heard mentioned from time to time on the news, thus making this an especially disturbing experience. Although I initially became very cynical and pessimistic, I quickly learned that this type of attitude was not only counterproductive in dealing with life and with patients, but was also very depressing. Eventually, I overcame this frustration, and have learned never to take one's own security, well-being, and confidence for granted. This experience helped me mature as a person, allowing me to understand how frustrating it must be for patients to overcome some of their own physical adversities that have often been inflicted upon them through no fault of their own.

> Be careful with intimate psychological disclosure.

> Makes the effects of a mugging relevant to career.

Example #2. This applicant uses a barebones description of a patient experience to demonstrate her appreciation of the unparalleled access that physicians have to their patients' intimate lives. More detail, however, would give her description some muscle.

In my second year of medical school I spent one afternoon each week with a primary care physician in San Francisco's Castro district. The practice specialized in caring for HIV-positive homosexual men. In addition to learning about the health care and social issues of this population, the patients and I grew comfortable with each other as I worked to earn their trust. The privilege of health care providers to share difficult times and confidential information with patients was clearly illustrated to me when after an interview a patient remarked, "You know, you're the only woman I've ever talked to about this."

> Functional summary of volunteer experience.

> Choice quote at end adds warmth.

Example #3. This applicant in family medicine makes a basic cultural and human observation through a touching yet humorous experience in an overcrowded Kenyan hospital. The richness of prose is matched by the complexity and maturity of thought behind her observations.

I found the explanation for my surprising happiness one night in an unusual way. At 3 AM I was called to the wards to admit a young woman

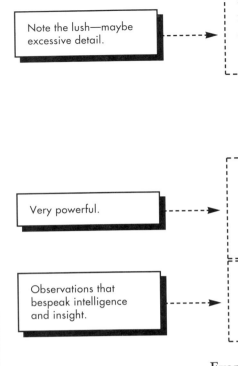

Note the lush—maybe excessive detail.

and arrived to find her comatose, moaning and rocking on her half of a rickety cot. I examined her, hung IV quinine for likely cerebral malaria, did a lumbar puncture, and put down an NG tube as the entire ward of sick women gravely watched the proceedings, their faces eerily illuminated by my penlight, the only source of light. Last to do was the Foley catheter, but try as I might I could not locate the woman's urethra. One of the nurses began to giggle—just a little giggle. I began to giggle. The women on the ward began to smile through their fevers, then chuckle. Soon the entire ward was laughing, great guffaws resounding through that miserable ward. I understood immediately. There was nothing vindictive or belittling in our laughter. On some unspoken group level, really a cultural level, we were pulling together to survive, transcending the almost unbearably hopeless human suffering. No one of us as an individual could hope to escape, but together, as a group, through this laughter—symbolic of some human universal, some common denominator, we stood a chance of retaining our dignity, our perspective, our optimism. Thinking about this moment afterwards, and, indeed, about my whole experience at Mogashi Hospital, I have come to realize the crucial role that cultural constructs—shared belief systems, mutual ways of reacting to circumstances, family, friends, rituals, society—play in an individual's life. . . .

Very powerful.

Observations that bespeak intelligence and insight.

Example #4.   Anecdotes about patients are commonly used to highlight an applicant's intelligence and compassion among other traits. Such accounts should, however, be used with discretion. Following is an example that works very well on the first read. However, the story starts to fall apart when you try to understand it on a deeper level. Compare this paragraph to the previous passage; note how much less involved you are in this story. There aren't enough telling details to bring the experience to life. Finally, the "lessons" the writer draws do not seem to unfold from her particular story.

During the first week of my outpatient medicine clerkship I met Miss G, a 65-year-old woman who came to the clinic for a routine health assessment. During the course of her evaluation, I obtained a screening mammogram which unfortunately revealed a spiculated mass suggestive of malignancy. For the first time in her life, Miss G faced the possibility of a diagnosis of cancer and realized she must come to terms with her own mortality. For the first time in my life, I found myself looking into the eyes of a patient, trying to be honest and kind while conveying bad news. It was a moment I remember well. I saw Miss G in clinic on several occasions over the ensuing weeks. Although she usually came to see me for health maintenance needs, we invariably turned to her concerns about breast cancer. She approached her fears with remarkable courage and stoicism, finally surrendering to tears of relief when her biopsy was found to be benign. I experienced both a sense of loss and a wonderful feeling of fulfillment when the months in the clinics came to an end. In retrospect, Miss G taught me more about illness, therapy, and what makes a patient "feel better" than I had learned in all of my classes.

Writer must have made a connection with the patient, but the message is not clear.

Avoid criticizing "all my classes," as the reader probably teaches one.

Strong Finishes

Example #1. This is an example of a strong finish, somewhat compromised by overuse of the first person singular. The applicant efficiently states his professional and personal goals, highlights notable personal qualities, and sets forth his expectations for residency training—all within five sentences. Unfortunately, each one starts with an "I."

> At UCSF I have experienced tremendous personal growth and have clarified my professional goals. I am committed to developing pragmatic multidisciplinary approaches to improving the quality and delivery of health care in the United States. Personally, I desire to provide compassionate and technically excellent medical care to patients from all walks of life. I will bring to residency energy, enthusiasm, integrity and ability. I expect a challenging, rich environment in which to learn and practice good medicine.

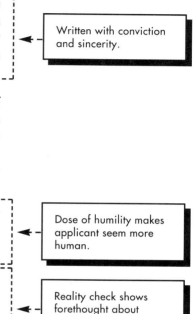

Very concise.

Written with conviction and sincerity.

Example #2. Many applicants finish with a "ready for anything" type of statement without convincing the reader that they understand what they're getting themselves into. This applicant takes an honest look at the challenges ahead and her ability to meet them. In addition, she balances discussions of her career plans with a glimpse into her personal life. We see how the interplay between work and leisure maintains her balance and stamina.

> I know I have set high goals for myself: clinician, educator, and health advocate. The majority of the time I find working with underserved populations extremely rewarding; however, it can also be emotionally demanding. I have profound admiration for family physicians who have devoted their life to this work. I often grapple with the question of what will enable me to sustain this commitment for a lifetime. The combination of working at an individual level to address health needs and at a more macroscopic level to affect health policy is synergistic for me—each inspires my work in the other. On a personal level, I find my time away from medicine rejuvenating as well. Spending time backpacking, gardening, or being with friends and family enables me to return to work refreshed. Being a physician entails personal sacrifice and dedication, and I am eager to begin the challenge.

Dose of humility makes applicant seem more human.

Reality check shows forethought about career plans.

Example #3. Female applicants in specialties traditionally dominated by men face special challenges. This surgery applicant injects some machismo into her career discussion/conclusion. Surgery training is often considered a rite of passage. She deals with possible concerns about her commitment to the specialty in the typical surgeon manner—head on. The applicant declares that she can handle anything that surgery training can dish out. In any other specialty, this chest-beating may appear ridiculous. Here her audacity earns respect. It only goes to show that in surgery attitude may be as important as ability.

> The requirements for a surgeon are stringent. Steady hands and a sharp scalpel do not make a surgeon; neither does pure surgical knowledge. Intellectual achievement and community involvement are not enough

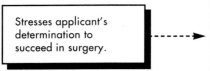

Stresses applicant's determination to succeed in surgery.

either. A candidate must be equipped with a true sense of commitment to be eligible for a career in surgery. My goals are simple: to learn constantly, so that, in turn, I may teach and heal. The dream of a career in surgery is no longer the naive one sparked first by my father's anecdotes. I am ready to accept the challenges and rigorous demands that accompany a surgeon's life.

SAMPLE PERSONAL STATEMENTS

In the following pages, we have reproduced some successful personal statements in their entirety, edited only to protect the applicant's identity. Most of the applicants behind these statements matched at top-flight institutions across the country. Once again, commentary is based on the observations of several residency directors, personal statement coaches, and a professional editor.

Personal Statement #1.   The writer of the following statement left a career in neuroscience research to pursue pediatric neurology. Her statement effectively addresses reasons for delaying medical school, disliking graduate training, and then entering medical school—answering directly the questions a director would have about an older applicant. The essay reads very naturally. Self-effacing humor and enthusiasm for the specialty inflect the essay and compensate for other shortcomings. The essay would have been improved, however, if the applicant had toned down her remarks about her love for the specialty.

When I first entered Oberlin College in 1980 I wanted to go into medicine—it took me 11 years to get there. When I first applied to medical school I thought about pediatric neurology—fortunately, it has not taken me another 11 years. During my third year pediatrics clerkship, I told one of my best friends from college (who is now a primary care attending) that I absolutely loved going to work every day and that I was amazed at how much fun it was to "play with" your patients. Her response was that I could have children of my own and I didn't *need* to go into a field of medicine just to "play with kids." As I continued to love every minute of my other pediatric rotations, I began to realize that of course I didn't *need* to, but that I certainly *could* if it was what I enjoyed the most and what I seemed to do the best.

> Good motivation.

When I was in college, I initially put off medicine for entirely the wrong reasons: I hated the competition of the premeds, I could not imagine studying non-stop, and I did not want to stay up all night every 3 to 4 days for years of my life. Instead, I knew that I wanted to study the brain, I had two wonderful role models in my psychobiology career, I got my thesis published, and I headed to graduate school looking forward to a career in neuroscience research. But I feel fortunate now that my 6 years in a graduate program in experimental neuropsychology at UCSD showed me that a career in research by itself was not enough.

> Appropriate exploration of reasons for entering first career.

The turning point was deeply personal. My 4-month-old niece was diagnosed with a grade 4 glioblastoma multiforme at the start of my fourth year. I remember sitting in the ICU waiting room at Denver Children's trying to concentrate on a paper related to my dissertation and realizing that what I was studying would never be directly helpful to this beautiful little child or to the rest of my family. It was then that I focused on why I had not been truly satisfied with my graduate experience—something was missing. And I came to realize that what was missing is the very thing that I need and want most from my career—direct application of my work. My personality needs more instant gratification than full-time research was bound to give me. In fact, the only

> Dramatizes her shift in values.

gratification that I did seem to be getting routinely in graduate school was through teaching. I loved the interaction with students, the challenge of being an effective communicator, and the sense of responsibility toward the students, all of which are integral parts of being a successful teacher. I received the Distinguished Teacher Award in 1992 and was subsequently appointed to the teaching assistant consultant position responsible for training all the new TAs in the psychology department. Unfortunately, in much of academia, teaching is not as valued a commodity as it should be, and I was constantly made to feel that I was spending "too much time and effort" teaching. As for my research efforts, I am fortunate enough to have experienced the thrill that comes from finding the predicted effects during the final data analysis of my dissertation project, but I know that this thrill would be magnified 10 times if the research had been clinically applicable. I also realized that ultimately I wanted more out of my interaction with patients than having them as research subjects. My experience in medical school has taught me that I was right, there is nothing more rewarding than direct patient care—no matter how challenging it can be. The fact that a career in academic medicine combines the patient care, teaching, and clinical research that I value so much makes me realize how lucky I am to have found this path.

Despite the fact that it was a little disconcerting to turn 30 during my first year of medical school in a class whose mean age was 23, and that it may seem a little harder for me to stay up all night than for my 25-year-old classmates, I have never regretted my path. I feel that the life experience gained from my year as a social worker working with pregnant and parenting teens, and my years in graduate school have contributed immeasurably to my learning of medicine. I knew better during first and second year what was really important—not the grades that I received, but rather how well I could learn to apply that knowledge to a clinical setting. I can also look at the frustrated and angry parents of a sick child and understand a little better what they are going through by applying my experience with my sister and niece.

For a short time during my third year I allowed myself to be steered toward adult neurology by eminent senior faculty members, but I knew there was something in my heart that would not let me make a final career decision until I had experienced child neurology. I went into it with mixed feelings. Another friend who was finishing her pediatrics residency had told me that she had considered doing a neurology fellowship, but thought that it was "too depressing" . . . so she went into oncology instead. I must admit that this scared me. But I knew after only a few days that this was what I was meant to do. I enjoyed every patient interaction I had—the 14-year-old with a static encephalopathy and an intractable seizure disorder, the perfectly normal 4-year-old who came for follow-up after a "bonk" on the head, and the 8-year-old with sudden onset of cranial nerve palsies of still unknown etiology. My learning curve was vertical and I went to sleep every night with Dr. Bruce Silverstein's text on my bed, and then was fortunate enough to have the opportunity to ask him questions in clinic in the morning.

Integrates awards into paragraph on interests.

Light-hearted acknowledgment that medicine is a second career.

Demonstrates how maturity works in applicant's favor.

Humor works surprisingly well here.

Many people have told me how lucky I am to have found a field that I am so enthusiastic about, that to fall so completely in love with something is what everybody hopes for. I knew that day that I went to Toys R Us (post-call) to buy a koosh ball to test visual fields and small plastic toys to test manual dexterity, and the night at 4 AM when I sat in a rocker to console a methadone baby in the nursery before going to bed for that all-important 2 hours' sleep that they were right.

You can chill; we know you like the specialty.

Personal Statement #2. The applicant has done a terrific job making her enthusiasm and convictions visible to us. The introduction is unevenly written, but the decision to launch the essay with a set of reasons for specializing in pediatrics makes the essay focused and direct from the start. In the middle two paragraphs, the applicant's extensive community activities are well described. Overall, the essay is solid and persuasive.

The writer scraps a superfluous introduction.

Good motivation.

"Most rewarding experiences": Good way of organizing paragraph.

Of the many contributing factors in my decision to pursue a career in pediatrics, the opportunity for patient education stands out as the most influential. During my clinical clerkships, I discovered many fields to be intriguing and learned from, as well as enjoyed, many aspects of each. It became clear, however, that the rotations providing more patient contact and continuity of care were the most fulfilling. My memories of third-year clerkships are of explaining cardiac catheterization to help allay fears, diagramming reasonable schedules of discharge medications, and discussing puberty with girls beginning their development. Thus, choosing a field became not merely a determination of what I found to be intellectually challenging, but a selection of the role I wished to play in delivering health care to my patients. Pediatrics as a specialty allows the most interaction with patients and their families and affords perhaps the broadest role for the physician, including that of child advocate/social activist, health educator, family friend and role model. Here, colleagues are interested in a patient's adoption history and school performance, and time can be scheduled solely for the purpose of STD teaching.

In my own educational experiences I have been blessed with supportive teachers who were also excellent role models. I was awarded the opportunity to enter a research laboratory as a high school student largely due to the commitment of a chemistry teacher and the generosity of a pharmacologist. This led to an aspiration to run my own laboratory with a program for future students. In college, a biochemistry professor's encouragement allowed me to pursue an individual project resulting in a publication. Perhaps as a means to reciprocate, I became involved in the local community. I performed the majority of my volunteer work through Alpha Phi Omega, a coeducational service fraternity affiliated with the Boy Scouts of America. Typical activities of the organization were Easter egg hunts for the county's foster children, creating a haunted house every Halloween at the Salvation Army, and providing aid in the aftermath of a local earthquake. Other community-oriented projects included tutoring of Chinatown youths on academic warning. As examples of Asians in college, the tutors also assumed roles of "big siblings" to help the students bridge cultural gaps and to encourage exploration of life opportunities outside the inner city. These activities eventually led me to realize that medicine, with its emphasis on service, would be the more satisfying career for me.

In medical school, I continued my community activities as time permitted. The two most rewarding experiences were that of teaching at a middle school and of organizing a series of talks for fellow preprofessional students. A few classmates and I taught middle schoolers through a program (Med Teach) coordinated by the medical school and the local school district. We had tremendous fun creating lesson plans for 3 classes each week, selecting different topics and styles of presentation for each age group. In addition to short traditional lectures, we often added interactive sessions such as class "Jeopardy" or "pin the organ on the body." One of our lessons on the eye even included group dissection of bovine eyeballs. This interest eventually grew to include the education of fellow classmates. As the community outreach chairperson for the Asian Health Caucus, I wanted medical professionals to learn about the special cultural as well as medical characteristics of the Asian patient (eg, population differences in disease prevalence and drug tolerances). This idea of hosting a single lecture on an Asian health topic was discussed with friends, many of whom voiced wishes for similar talks on other cultural groups. Thus sprouted the day-long Multicultural Health Forum which explored various cultures and their relevant health issues with speakers from different institutions. Moreover, I was able to secure sponsorship from the department of Psychiatry and develop the forum as a credited class with availability to all pre-professional schools including those of pharmacy, nursing, dentistry, and medicine.

The writer describes a project from start to finish, showing that she can follow through.

I am eager to maintain my interest in teaching, both through patient education and through involvement with medical student training— knowing well the difference an interested resident can make in the medical student experience. Because of this factor, there was never any doubt that I would be best suited for a university based/affiliated pediatrics residency program. I currently anticipate a career in general pediatrics and therefore desire a well-rounded program with strong training in primary care. However, infectious disease and genetics are two areas which I wish to further explore with the option of possible advanced training.

Personal Statement #3. This applicant in plastic and reconstructive surgery does a particularly good job detailing research interests without overloading the reader. Note that she rarely has to discuss her interest in plastic surgery in abstract terms—specificity makes this essay work. Through careful attention to her prose, the applicant shows that she cares about her future career in plastics.

As a volunteer anatomy and pathology laboratory instructor, each year I am faced with a new set of students, unpredictable new group dynamics, and ultimately new challenges for presenting material. At times such as these, I truly appreciate the remarkable plasticity of the human mind. A principle taught to me by my own college anatomy instructor, who influenced my career by teaching me *how to teach,* often comes to mind: "Answering a confused student's question with the same words repeatedly is like trying to cut paper by hitting it with a hammer over and over. Instead, trash the hammer and get a pair of scissors," she said, "or start tearing." Through the years, I have learned that effectual communication entails transmission of the understanding that you possess to others, so that they now also understand and are stimulated to think. This requires flexibility and patience, a good understanding and organization of the material, and a high degree of enthusiasm on the part of the teacher. While some of these attributes are inherent in my character, others have been learned and improved upon with every new enterprise.

It is a similar challenge that attracts me to the field of plastic and reconstructive surgery where often there are situations when operative procedures are modified to accommodate a patient's situation. Whether there is a paucity of soft tissue in one area, an abundance of skin in another, or a lack of bone due to destruction or congenital absence, the human body can be made plastic much like the mind modifying the procedures. I welcome and look forward to a lifetime career of meeting these types of challenges creatively in both the adult and pediatric populations, always keeping in mind aesthetics, prognosis, functionality, and the patient's wishes.

Creativity extends to the area of research, which together with teaching, draws me toward a career in academics. To offer a patient an objective list of therapeutic alternatives requires an active hand in contributing to basic and clinical sciences while keeping abreast of the most recent advancements. As an undergraduate in kinesiology at the University of Miami Biomechanics Laboratory, I investigated the recruitment pattern of the medial and lateral gastrocnemius heads in the cat across a continuum of postural and movement demands. To further study pathophysiologic mechanisms of diseases in light of a surgical subspecialty, I completed a Post-Sophomore fellowship with the Florida State Department of Anatomic Pathology, gaining familiarity with frozen biopsy criteria and processing, histologic examination of surgical specimens, special stains, cytologic interpretation, and fresh anatomic dissection during autopsies. Interested in diseases of the musculoskeletal system, I researched a new monoclonal antibody, O13, directed against the p30/32 gene of Ewing's sarcoma and its cross reactivities with other small round blue cell tumors. Possessing a special interest in

Effective use of an anecdote to illustrate a point.

Interesting analogy—plasticity as a parallel between teaching and reconstructive surgery.

Good use of specific details.

pediatric orthopedics, I participated in many of the Toland Hospital for Crippled Children activities over the course of 3 years, including an anesthesia clerkship, contributing to research conducted in the Gait Laboratory, participating in rounds and conferences, and observing a variety of orthopedic surgeries, the majority involving congenital hand abnormalities. It was here that I met Dr. Kathryn Douglass of Baylor University, who introduced me to the notion of approaching a possible hand fellowship from the direction of plastic surgery. Now, with my current interest in plastic and reconstructive surgery, I am presently exploring with Dr. William Schrock at Baylor University the potential of capitalizing upon the angiogenic properties of fibroblast growth factor in the creation of flaps for larger wound coverage secondary to burns or other major trauma.

The writer's name-dropping is effective because she substantiates the references and explains their significance.

Plasticity, also, is a key virtue during any residency. I am quick to learn new theories and techniques, and able to work well with a wide variety of patient and medical staff personalities. These attributes, coupled with patience and a good sense of humor, have been instrumental in my growth thus far and will continue to be the basic foundation of my philosophy for success in plastic and reconstructive surgery.

Personal Statement #4. This very capable statement shows a strong sense of purpose while reviewing several past accomplishments. It offers another example of how to make an applicant's interests appear coherent and consistent.

Jumbled introduction; jumps from fact to fact too quickly.

While growing up in Chicago, I was curious about the city's economic and social segregation, and what could be done to change it. As an English major at Ohio University, I originally intended to teach high school in the inner city, where I felt I might have an impact on education for disadvantaged students. During that time I founded one of the first inner-city Girl Scout troops in Akron and led a troop of 30 girls for 4 years. As the girls began to trust me, they started to ask questions about pregnancy, drugs, and STDs. Although I greatly enjoyed my role as an impromptu health educator, I sensed the futility of providing education without other health resources. Most of these girls received medical care for acute needs only; very few had access to regular primary care. I became increasingly aware of the need for partnership between health education and primary health care. My interest in these issues generated my desire for a career in medicine. I am particularly attracted to Family Practice because it integrates the roles of clinician, educator, and health advocate into the role of physician.

During medical school my primary goal was to develop my clinical skills; however, it was important to me to continue to work with underserved populations to reaffirm my reason for studying medicine. After my first year, I received a scholarship from the Ohio Valley Homelessness Project to study health care access among homeless people.

Impressive achievement, described in detail.

I became acutely aware of the impact of homelessness on health status, and this motivated me to involve other students in this issue. To this end, I helped found a free clinic for homeless people in the 2300 on Main homeless shelter. The Ohio University Students' Homeless Clinic is entirely run by students and volunteer physicians. Since 1991, over 200 students and 30 physicians have provided over 2500 patient visits free of charge. In conjunction with establishing the clinic I also helped develop an elective, currently in its fourth year, on health issues among the homeless. I have remained extremely involved in running the homeless clinic since its inception and currently serve on the Board of Directors. In 1994, I received the Margaret Dawson Award for Outstanding Commitment to Social Action and Social Justice. This is the single award presented at graduation from the School of Public Health.

Sage and succinct.

Working at the clinic constantly reminds me of both my powers and limitations as a future physician. Homeless people have myriad physical, social, and economic factors affecting their health; many have problems far too complex to resolve in a single visit. At first, I was frustrated if patients would come to the clinic requesting moisturizing cream or cough syrup, but were resistant to discussing what I deemed more serious problems—such as substance abuse or hypertension. Eventually, I learned that by first addressing the patient's presenting complaint we could establish trust, which might form the basis for a more

Reinforces primary care philosophy.

continuous relationship. These long-term relationships are what I value most about being a physician. This was affirmed for me in my year-long longitudinal clinic at Swanson Hill Health Center in 1993 as well as during my current longitudinal clinic at the AGH Family Health Center. Through these experiences I have had the opportunity to work with patients on health-related behaviors such as smoking cessation. While trying to change behavior often seems futile or frustrating at a single visit, following patients over a year has shown me the value of incremental change toward healthier lifestyles. The challenges and the rewards of working in this setting reconfirmed my interest in Family Practice.

Dealing with underserved patients' day-to-day medical needs stimulated my interest in studying health care policy on a more global level. As a result, I took a year off between my third and fourth years to pursue a Master's degree in Public Health at Ohio University. My main focus was to examine the factors contributing to the shortage of primary-care physicians in underserved communities. I became convinced that changes in medical education could have an impact on the number of primary care physicians in underserved areas. Along these lines, I was active on a student-faculty committee whose goal was to integrate more primary care and women's health instruction into the curriculum. In addition, through the Department of Family Practice, I am currently researching how medical students' experiences in the homeless clinic affect their choice of a career in primary care and their interest in working with underserved populations. When this work is complete, I intend to submit it for publication.

I know I have set high goals for myself: clinician, educator, and health advocate. The majority of the time I find working with underserved populations extremely rewarding; however, it can also be emotionally demanding. I have profound admiration for family physicians who have devoted their life to this work. I often grapple with the question of what will enable me to sustain this commitment for a lifetime. The combination of working at an individual level to address health needs and at a more macroscopic level to affect health policy is synergistic for me—each inspires my work in the other. On a personal level, I find my time away from medicine rejuvenating as well. Spending time backpacking, gardening, or being with friends and family enables me to return to work refreshed. Being a physician entails personal sacrifice and dedication, and I am eager to begin the challenge.

The writer makes the year off seem a logical result of her passion for health care, not a deviation in any sense.

Somewhat weak; let your letter writer mention.

Personalizes the statement.

Gearing Up for Interviews

8

You can breathe a small sigh of relief when invitations for interviews start coming in. You have cleared the first major hurdle in the match process, and your foot is in the door of several programs at least. Now, how to maneuver the rest of yourself through the doorway.

HOW DO I PREPARE FOR THE INTERVIEW?

Good preparation for program interviews is essential to making the best impression. Being overtired, disorganized, inappropriately dressed, or upset about travel glitches can only hurt. In this chapter we will walk you through the stages of interview preparation.

Scheduling Interviews

Many program directors will tell you that the date of your interview should not make a difference; however, conventional wisdom favors choosing the latter half of the interview season, so that committee members will better recall your application during the ranking sessions. For many applicants, the crucial period is after Christmas.

As a result, during the peak interview months of January and February, last minute scheduling changes are very difficult. In addition, travel to the Northeast is especially unpredictable. The Blizzard of 1996 forced thousands of applicants to cancel or reschedule key interviews. If you are in an early match, you will be interviewing from September through December. Remember, if you want maximal flexibility in interview planning, you **must** turn in your applications early.

The interview process can be more grueling than you think. For starters, **don't schedule interviews too close together.** Space them at least 2 days apart so that you'll have time to travel, recuperate and digest information from the previous interview. Schedule the most competitive and desirable programs in the middle of your interview schedule. By then you should reach peak interview form without having lost your enthusiasm and energy (Figure 8–1). In fact, many applicants end up canceling interviews near the end of the season from pure fatigue. If you decide you do not want or cannot make an interview appointment, inform the program as far in advance as you

> INTERVIEWS LATER
> IN THE SEASON ARE
> MORE MEMORABLE BUT
> ARE ALSO MORE OF A HASSLE.

> SCHEDULE THE MOST
> COMPETITIVE AND YOUR
> MOST DESIRABLE PROGRAMS
> IN THE MIDDLE OF YOUR
> INTERVIEW SCHEDULE.

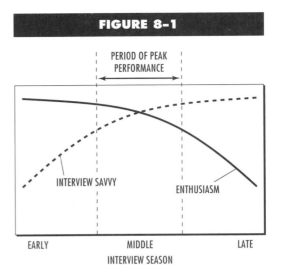

FIGURE 8-1

PERIOD OF PEAK PERFORMANCE

INTERVIEW SAVVY

ENTHUSIASM

EARLY · MIDDLE · LATE
INTERVIEW SEASON

Performance during interview season.

can, so that they can fill your interview slot with another applicant. It's simple courtesy. Bear in mind that reports of bad manners travel far in the small circle of residency program directors.

Try to arrange interviews in geographical clusters, so that you can easily drive between sites or take advantage of cheaper regional travel options (See the section "Planes, Trains, and Automobiles"). It is not inappropriate to politely request an interview at a specific program if you will be traveling to that general area for other interviews. Ask if rounds or a morning conference is a scheduled part of the day's activities. If not, ask if you can attend one or the other. Rounds/conferences are often one of the easiest and most useful ways to judge the style and caliber of a program.

Mock Interviews

When you hit the interview trail, you will want to be in fine shape. Real interviews are time-consuming and take serious effort to set up. **Never** treat a real interview as a practice session, even if it is at one of your less desirable programs. You never know how a visit will affect your rankings, especially if you end up bumping one of your lower-ranked choices to the top of your "most wanted" list.

After 4 years in school, however, anyone could lose their interviewing finesse. To get a little practice before the real thing, set up a mock interview with your career adviser or another faculty member in the department. Ideally, this person will be an active member of the selection committee in your specialty. Before you go in for your mock interview, review Chapter 9. Have your "interviewer" conduct a "tough" interview with hard questions, especially if he or she has a reputation as a "softy." Otherwise, he or she should treat you like any other candidate who walks through the door. Afterwards, your "interviewer" should give you detailed feedback on your ease/ confidence in handling the questions, the quality of your answers, and other personal qualities that you projected during the interview (eg, maturity, thoughtfulness, intelligence, ability to think quickly, etc).

If you want to squeeze even more feedback out of the ersatz interview, you can have it videotaped or audiotaped, and then review it with your "in-

ROUNDS AND CONFERENCES PROVIDE GLIMPSES OF THE PROGRAM'S SOUL.

terviewer." Try to evaluate yourself from his or her perspective. You can also simulate other aspects of the interview by coming to the "office" in full interview dress, carrying a folder of materials, and being forced to stew a few minutes outside with the secretary because the interviewer is currently with another applicant. Likewise, you can assemble as complete an application file as possible, have the "interviewer" review it, and ask you questions based on your file. For the truly obsessive-compulsive, there are even professionals who can play the interviewer, videotape the session, and coach you to a fine-tuned performance.

Doing Your Homework for the Road

A few days before any actual interview, call the institution to confirm the date, time, location, and interviewers. If you have any of their names, build on this knowledge. Is your interviewer a researcher, a clinician, a house officer, or an administrator? Then get to work: (1) Call up local contacts (ie, graduates from your school currently in the program), or ask the program's administrative assistant about the interviewer's specialty, personality, etc.; (2) Run a MEDLINE search on the interviewer(s) and read their abstracts. Discover mutual interests to discuss. For the Internet savvy applicant, use Alta Vista (http://www.altavista.digital.com) to run a Web or Usenet search on the interviewer's name. The goal is not to appear political or "calculated," but to be prepared to highlight any strengths you have that might appeal to the interviewer. Even if what you learn does not come up in conversation, you will gain a psychological advantage just from knowing something about the interviewer. He or she already knows a great deal about you; doing your homework offers you a chance to even the playing field a little. In preparation for the interview, you want to organize the following information about each program (Figure 8–2).

Place all this material in a labeled folder. If you have time, review this material and jot down questions and concerns that come to mind for that program. You should also create a folder of your own application materials (Figure 8–3).

Of course, the residency director will also have this information—plus your application—in front of her when she interviews you, all of which is fair game.

LEVEL THE INTERVIEW PLAYING FIELD BY LEARNING ABOUT YOUR INTERVIEWERS.

FIGURE 8–2

☐ The *First Aid for the Match* program evaluation worksheet
☐ The full FREIDA printout
☐ Informational brochures and pamphlets
☐ A photocopy of your application
☐ Any notes that you picked up from faculty house staff or fellow students
☐ For the research oriented, a MEDLINE search of your interviewers' publications
☐ A color photograph of yourself if one was not sent to the program

Checklist for program information.

FIGURE 8–3

☐ The dean's letter
☐ Copies of any letters of recommendation that were made available to you
☐ Copies of your transcript(s)
☐ Your CV
☐ Your personal statement (especially if you personalized your statement)
☐ Reprints of any noteworthy publications
☐ A copy of your *First Aid for the Match* worksheet of application requirements

Checklist for folder of application materials.

Interview Attire and Grooming

General Tips. Remember, you are trying to get a job as a doctor, so dress like one. Both men and women should dress conservatively but stylishly. Clothing and shoes should be comfortable, since most interviews will include tours of the facility. You might want to bring a small leather briefcase or a neat folder containing blank paper, pen, and extra copies of your CV and personal statement. Since most of the interviews will be conducted in the late fall or winter, dress for warmth, particularly if you are interviewing at programs in the Snowbelt. Always ask another person to inspect your appearance in your interview suit to make sure that you project a professional, polished image. Don't forget to schedule a haircut or trim before you take your show on the road, particularly if your hair loses all shape or style when overdue for a trim. Finally, if you do use fragrance or aftershave lotion, go easy with the dosage. You want to be remembered for your "stylish young doctor" look, not for filling the room or elevator with a thick cloud of fragrance.

Just for Men. Don't assume that your suits from your medical school interviewing days still fit. Try them on several months in advance. If they no longer fit or are not in style and cannot be easily altered, consider a shopping trip. If you want custom-tailored suits, get measured for them at least 2 months before your interviews begin. If you buy ready-made suits, tell the salesperson that you are looking for interview suits. If you cannot stand the traditional black, brown and navy, consider olive. In any case, remain with a conservative but classy cut; this is not the time to experiment with avant-garde designer labels. Your shirts should also be conservative in style and color, and made of good-quality material.

Two suits should be adequate for most interview trips. Each suit should be good for two or three interviews. Alternate your suits to let the other suit air out and shed its wrinkles. When there is a break in the interview schedule, you can have the suits dry-cleaned. You might want to pack a portable iron and a lint brush for trips.

Men with fast growing beards: it's not a bad idea to carry a razor so that you can shave right before afternoon interview sessions. A five o'clock shadow can take the edge off your sharp professional image.

Just for Women. Unfortunately, women's styles change so quickly that the suits you bought before medical school will probably look dated. Unless you've purchased a suit within the past 2 years, now is the time to splurge

AVOID LETHAL DOSES OF PERFUME OR AFTERSHAVE.

and invest in one or two new suits for the interview trips. Although there are many stylish pants suits out there, conservative wisdom prefers the classically cut skirt and jacket ensemble. The jacket must be long-sleeved. The skirt should fall just below, or just above, the knee. When you try the skirt on, march around the dressing room area. If the skirt won't allow you to stride freely, it's wrong for a professional outfit. You'll be doing a lot of walking on your interviews, and you need a skirt that won't hobble you.

AVOID THE "DRUG REP" LOOK.

Although women have more choices than men in suit colors, it's a good idea to stay away from overly bright colors and busy patterns. Similarly, your blouse should be classic in cut, with a neckline that is not too low, and in a color and texture complementary to the suit. Generally, suits made of wool or linen/cotton blends travel best, with the fewest wrinkles and the best fabric weight to adapt to changing weather conditions. Be prepared to spend several days shopping for the right suit. If you have the time, you may want to take your new purchase to a men's tailor for alterations. Unlike men, women are generally not accustomed to having off-the-rack suits altered for a perfect fit, but when 3 or 4 years of your future are at stake, it may well be worth the extra cost. Professional alterations are especially important if you are not a standard size.

CONSIDER PROFESSIONAL ALTERATIONS.

It's difficult to walk the fine line of looking professional and still looking feminine. The shoes that you will be wearing on interview trips should be comfortable, since there may be a lot of walking on slippery hospital floors. Generally, low-heeled pumps in a color complementary to your suits are best, with neutral-colored hosiery. Keep makeup and jewelry to a minimum. Unless you really need one, don't carry a handbag. Instead, opt for a leather attaché case to hold your papers, keys, makeup, and a comb or brush.

HOW CAN I TRAVEL INEXPENSIVELY?

Unfortunately, interviews will ding most of you for a lot of time and money. During the 1993–94 interview season, for example, students spent an average of 18 days away from medical school at their program interviews, and paid $1500 for application fees and travel expenses (Figures 8–4 and 8–5).

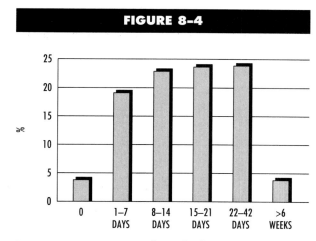

FIGURE 8–4

Days spent interviewing away from school.

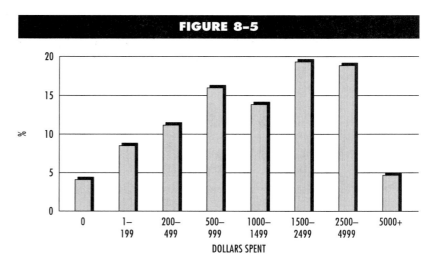

FIGURE 8-5

Amount in U.S. dollars spent applying and interviewing for residency positions.

It's possible in most cases to make travel arrangements for your interviews without razing your bank account. To some extent, the most cost-efficient means of transportation depends on geographical location. Some parts of the United States have better rail service than others. In some areas, a rented car may be your best option. The next section will introduce you to some ways to minimize your travel expenses.

Planes, Trains, and Automobiles

American Express Student Privileges: If you do not yet have an American Express card with student privileges, we recommend that you get one. At present, the AMEX student card comes with two coupons, good for heavily discounted travel on Continental Airlines. The coupons are well worth the $55 annual AMEX membership fee. Be sure to let AMEX know that you are a medical student when you enroll as a card member. As this book goes to press, the coupons allow you to purchase a round-trip ticket for $159 if you stay on one side of the Mississippi River. The cost is $239 if your travel takes you across it. You must make reservations less than 21 days in advance. That means that you can make last minute reservations if seats are still available in the appropriate fare class. In addition, you can currently take a companion with you at the same fare. If you are interviewing together as a couple, or if you can coordinate interviews with a friend, you can get extra mileage from the American Express/Continental coupons. Out of coupons? No problem. You can call AMEX for another set of coupons. For further information or to enroll in the Student Privileges program, call:

American Express Student Privileges
(800) 942-2639

AMA-MSS travel discounts: If you are a member of the AMA Medical Student Section, you can take advantage of modest discounts on Continental and Northwest airfares. Remember, however, that even with the discounts, the AMA-MSS air fares may not be your best deals. Check with your

DON'T LEAVE HOME
WITHOUT IT.

local travel agent. To get more information about AMA-MSS travel discounts, call:

> Continental Airlines
> (800) 468-7022, Reference ID# JM87WX
> Northwest Airlines
> (800) 328-1111, Reference ID# NS4BV

AMSA travel discounts: AMSA also offers its members some savings on air fares and car rentals through Travel One, AMSA's official travel agency. Check with your local travel agent to make sure that you're quoted the best deals going. To get updated information on AMSA travel discounts, call:

> Travel One
> (800) 800-9012

American Airlines Meeting Saver Fares for AAMC Student Residency Interview Program: Discounts of 5% and 10% on American Airlines fares are available to all medical students during the interview season. The discounts are not enormous; however, you can get them without coupons or membership in any organization. For more information, call:

> American Airlines Meeting Services
> (800) 433-1790; ask for STAR file #S-9255

Discount regional airlines: Given recent increased competition from low-fare airlines like Southwest, you can obtain very reasonable airfares when traveling regionally (Table 8–1). As with other airlines, tickets are cheapest with a 21-day advance purchase and a Saturday night stay. With discount airlines, you may encounter less choice in flight times and more stopovers.

Amtrak "All Aboard": Amtrak's "All Aboard" train travel program allows you three stops within a 45-day period. "All Aboard" divides the country into three geographic regions (Western, Central, Eastern). Fares, which start at $178, increase as you traverse more regions. For more information, call:

> AMTRAK
> (800) USA-RAIL

TABLE 8–1. Cheap airlines		
Airline	**Regions with Strong Coverage**	**Phone Number**
Alaska Airlines	West Coast	(800) 426-0333
America West	Southwest	(800) 235-9292
Frontier	Denver, West Coast, and Midwest	(800) 432-1359
Midway	Midwest and East Coast	(800) 446-4392
Midwest Express	Midwest	(800) 452-2022
Reno Air	Nevada and West Coast	(800) 736-6247
Southwest Airlines	West Coast, Midwest, South	(800) I-FLY-SWA
Tower Air	Coast-to-Coast	(800) 221-2500
United Shuttle	Both coasts	(800) SHUTTLE

East Coast light rail: Because the entire Eastern seaboard is well connected with light rail, rail is a viable alternative to driving, especially given distances of 200 miles or greater. Reasonable fares are available even with little advance reservation or none. To receive general rail schedules for the East Coast, call:

AMTRAK
(800) USA-RAIL

For the New York metropolitan area and Connecticut, call:

Metro-North
(800) 638-7646

In general, rail travel may be a more useful throwback than you think: you can use the time to review interview materials, rest, or catch up on other reading, none of which is possible when you drive.

Travel agencies: You can purchase a ticket directly through the airlines described earlier; or you can visit your local travel agency. Student-oriented discount travel agencies include STA Travel (800) 777-0112 and Let's Go Travel (800-5LETSGO). Travel agents have access to information about the lowest available airfares on all major airlines. Unfortunately, some discount airlines, like Southwest, are not listed on their computers. Their services are free to you, since their commissions are paid by the airlines. In general, try to purchase tickets 3 weeks in advance for the cheapest fares. Make sure the airport you fly into is the best airport in terms of price and distance from your program destination. You must balance the airfare with the time and cost of a taxi to your lodging.

Where to Stay

You will need to take overnight housing into account as part of your travel plans. It isn't always necessary to figure big bucks into your budget for this item; consider the following possibilities:

Free or low-cost accommodations arranged by the program: Some programs, especially primary care programs in the Midwest and East, will provide complimentary or discounted lodging at a nearby hotel or guest house. If your interview situation does not volunteer information about such arrangements, ask the administrative assistant if any are available.

Housing Extension Network (HEN): This housing network is a service provided by the Organization of Student Representatives, a section of the AAMC. Any medical school can participate in the network if at least eight medical students at that school are willing to house visiting applicants. Participating hosts need not be fourth-year students. One advantage of arranging housing through HEN, however, is that your host **might** be a fourth-year medical student who can give you the last (or latest) word on the program and the institution. If your school is a HEN participant, a directory of other participating schools and hosts with phone numbers and addresses is available through your student affairs office or class representative. If your school is not a part of HEN, bring the network to the attention of your class officers. For further information call:

AAMC
(202) 828-0682

For women—AMWA Bed & Breakfast Program: The American Medical Women's Association has a "Bed and Breakfast Program" for members traveling to residency interviews. A member calls AMWA and specifies her destination. AMWA then supplies her with a list of members in the area, mostly physicians who have agreed to provide short-term lodging for other members. The student is then responsible for making arrangements with the host. AMWA charges $10 for the referral service; the student pays her host an additional $15. To use the service or for more information, call or write:

American Medical Women's Association
801 North Fairfax Street, #400
Alexandria, VA 22314-1767
(703) 838-0500

Recent graduates: Some student affairs offices maintain lists of recent graduates and their residency programs. Not only are recent graduates at your target programs an invaluable source of information about the program, they might offer to put you up for a night when you visit.

Other applicants: On the interview trail, you often meet applicants from the schools and institutions that you will later be visiting. They may be friendly enough to offer you housing when you visit their home institution, or just show you around the evening before the interview. If they will also be visiting your school at some point, consider extending them the same courtesies.

Accommodations recommended by the program: If you are stumped for housing options or prefer more luxurious surroundings, you can always check out local hotels recommended by the program. Residency programs often make arrangements with a hotel to offer discounts if you mention that you are interviewing with them. This information is often included with written invitations for interviews. If you don't get the official word, you can ask the administrative assistant for suggestions.

Hotel Discounts: Hotel-discount companies that consolidate empty hotel rooms can offer you 20 to 70% off the regular rates if they make your arrangements (Table 8–2). Best availability is usually restricted to the major cities. Don't forget to ask about the cancellation policy before booking. In addition, after getting a rate on a given hotel, check with the hotel directly and find out: (1) its proximity to the residency program; and (2) whether an even lower price is available.

If you know that you'll be doing some significant traveling, consider enrolling in a program that can get you up to a 50% discount off regular hotel rates wherever you travel. The major programs usually include more than 2000 hotels worldwide (Table 8–3). To be eligible for the discount, you usually make a reservation with your membership card number. The discount rate may have limited availability, and sometimes requires a 30-day advance notice. If all goes well, you can end up pampered, save some money and save the highway-motel experience for later.

TABLE 8–2. Hotel-discount companies	
Company	**Number**
Hotel Reservations Network	(800) 964-6835
Quickbook	(800) 789-9887
Room Exchange	(800) 846-7000

TABLE 8–3. Some half-price hotel programs		
Program	**Membership Price**	**Number**
America at 50%	$19.95	(800) 248-2783
Encore	$49.95	(800) 638-0930
Entertainment Publications	$27.95 (national ed.)	(800) 445-4137

Budget-Priced Chains: Finally, you can simply go with a budget ho tel/motel chain. If the residency program is not helpful with names and numbers of nearby lodging, you can call any of these major chains (Table 8–4). When you make your reservation, ask about the room. Common con cerns include a non-smoking room, location in a quiet part of the hotel/mo tel, and a phone connection. And for security, is there a dead-bolt lock? A peephole in the door?

University Dorms. Many residency programs are located at colleges and universities which rent out empty dormitory rooms for $15 to $30 per

TABLE 8–4. Major budget hotel/motel chains	
Chain	**Number**
Budgets Inns	(800) 4-BUDGET
Clubhouse Inns	(800) CLUB-INN
Comfort Inns	(800) 4-CHOICE
Country Lodging	(800) 456-4000
Courtyard Marriott	(800) 321-2211
Days-Inns	(800) 325-2525
Econo Lodge	(800) 4-CHOICE
Fairfield Inn	(800) 228-2800
Friendship Inns	(800) 4-CHOICE
Hampton Inn	(800) HAMPTON
HoJo Inn	(800) 654-2000
Holiday Inn Express	(800) HOLIDAY
La Quinta	(800) 531-5900
Motel 6	(505) 891-6161
Ramada Ltd.	(800) 2-RAMADA
Red Roof Inns	(800) THE-ROOF
Super8	(800) 800-8000
Travelodge	(800) 255-3050

night. Unfortunately, programs sometimes neglect to mention such accommodations in their brochures.

Handy Travel Tips

Lastly, we offer a few additional pointers to make your interview trip as smooth as possible:

1. Plan to arrive at your accommodations no later than the afternoon of the day before your interview. This will give you a chance to get oriented, adjust to time zone differences, and handle any unexpected mishaps (eg, lost luggage). If you are planning to fly out the day of the interview, check with the departmental secretary to make sure that there are no further events scheduled for later that day. About departures: in general, it is better to leave later in the day if possible, so that you can have extra time to talk to house staff and faculty, or to see more of the hospital and facilities.

2. When flying, try to take everything as carry-ons. You can bypass the crowded airport counter for a gate check-in and eliminate the risk of the airline losing your luggage. We suggest a durable garment bag or a roll-aboard suit carrier for your interview clothing. If you must travel heavy, at least pack your interview essentials (eg, program interview materials, application materials, and interview suit) in a carry-on.

3. Pick up an updated discount travel guide. A particularly useful book (it saved one of us, stranded at La Guardia, several hundred dollars on airfare) is *Travel Smarts: Getting the Most for Your Travel Dollar* (Globe Pequot Press) by Teison and Dunnan. This guide, or a similar book by Consumer Reports, will stretch your travel dollar and minimize traveling hassles without sacrificing comfort.

4. If you plan on driving to most of your destinations, get a good U.S. map/road atlas for trip planning. Carry a pocket local map for each city you visit, or tear out the detail pages from an inexpensive road atlas. If you belong to the American Automobile Association (AAA), call or visit your local office once you know your itinerary. Membership privileges usually include free road maps and customized routing advice. It's also worth inquiring about discounts on car rentals and lodging; many AAA clubs offer coupons for these services. And if you should have car problems en route, an AAA card can often save you much more than the cost of the annual membership fee.

    Before you set off, have your car properly winterized and tuned; ask the service station attendant to check your fluids, tire pressure, and replace your windshield wipers if necessary. Be sure to keep your car registration, inspection and insurance papers, and auto club materials in the glove compartment. If you don't already have one for your car, buy a flashlight and batteries—particularly if you will be driving at night.

5. If you have the time, the interview season can be a great way to mix business and pleasure. You can squeeze in some sightseeing if you have more than a day between interviews. You get to unwind between interviews and learn more about the local attractions in the vicinity of the program.

ARRIVE EARLY; LEAVE LATE

6. Be sure to check local weather conditions in the city where you will be interviewing before you set off. This is especially important if you are traveling to an unfamiliar part of the country, or if you are flying to a region with an exteme climate.

REFERENCES

University of California at San Francisco School of Medicine, *The Next Step: Your Guide to Residency*. San Francisco: University of California at San Francisco, 1995.
Teison H, Dunnan N: *Travel Smarts*. Old Sanbroot, CT: The Globe Pequot Press, 1995.

Interview Day

9

WHAT SHOULD I DO THE DAY BEFORE THE INTERVIEW?

By the time you set out on your interview trip, you will want to feel as confident and well prepared as possible. If you have taken our advice in Chapter 8, and planned your arrival for the afternoon before the day of your interview, you will have enough time for these necessary last-minute preparations.

Review the Program. Pull out your file on the program you are visiting, including its brochures, your application, the FREIDA printout, etc. Next, review the file of application materials that you had sent to all programs. Try to anticipate interview questions based on your application materials. This step is especially important if your application has some weaknesses. Then make notes on the information you will need to complete your Program Evaluation Worksheet for that program.

Logistics. Review your interview itinerary if the program sent you one. Next, orient yourself in the city or town, locate the program offices in relation to your lodging, and make transportation arrangements if you aren't within walking distance of your morning destination. Then, double-check your wardrobe and attaché case; make sure that nothing is missing or damaged.

TYPICAL EVENTS OF AN INTERVIEW VISIT

No matter what specialty you choose, the visits usually follow the chronology listed below. The interview proper is discussed on pages 135–142. Each segment of the visit represents a different opportunity to learn more about the program, as well as another chance to make a positive impression on the committee members. Be alert; recalibrate your eyes and ears to make the most of each situation, and tailor your questions and responses accordingly. Tune in to your intuition as well; your "gut feelings" may be sending you important warning signals.

Preinterview Social Events

On the evening before the interview day, programs often invite applicants to dinner with members of the house staff. These meals are typically meant to provide an opportunity for applicants to learn more about the training program in an environment free from the scrutiny of selection committee members. Dress is casual, but avoid jeans and shorts. However, do not be fooled by the relaxed atmosphere; the selection committee usually includes residents and interns. In addition, remember that any strong impression that you leave on any member of the house staff, whether positive or negative, will be communicated to the selection committee.

Introductions

ORIENT YOURSELF IMMEDIATELY TO THE INTERVIEW SCHEDULE.

In the morning of the interview day, you and your fellow applicants will gather in a conference room, where you will (usually) receive a folder containing an itinerary of the day's events, a name tag, a brochure about the training program; and (possibly) call schedules, a summary of benefits, a list of current house officers, and typical house officer rotation schedules. Give the day's schedule priority; read through it carefully, making mental notes of times and places for your interviews. Scan the rest of the packet at your discretion. On interview day itself, pretty color brochures are almost always useless. Save those for later.

After everyone has gathered, you may be addressed by the program director or the chair of the department. It may seem like a routine formality, but give the speaker your full attention. You will usually be able to read the guiding philosophy of the program "between the lines" of the address. As you listen, keep in mind that the preaching and philosophy of the residency director and the department chair heavily shape the program. You will need to ask yourself whether the "shape" of this particular program is compatible with your outlook and goals.

Tour of Facilities

Most program visits include a tour of the facilities, led by a resident or intern. At programs with multiple training sites, you will usually tour just one hospital in the system, so don't forget to ask questions about the other sites. If there is something you really want to see, your guide will usually be happy to show it to you (Table 9–1). If you can, stay close to your guide; you won't hear anything in the back of the pack. Because your tour leader has to speak so much, you often pick up more unfiltered sentiments and honest opinions than at any other time during your visit.

TABLE 9-1. Sights to see on a program tour.		
Must See	**Should See**	**Might See**
Wards	Emergency room	Surrounding city
ICU	Cafeteria	Fitness facilities
Surgical suites	Library/computer resources	Child care facilities
Call rooms		

Morning Rounds/Conferences

Every interview itinerary should allow you to see the house staff in action, whether on rounds or in conference. Otherwise, you simply will not get the full picture. Rounds and conferences allow you to gauge the enthusiasm of the house staff, the breadth of knowledge displayed, and the quality of interaction among house officers, staff and faculty. Pay particular attention to the post-call house officers, who tend to be forthcoming in their sleep-deprived state. Your challenge then is to distinguish between grousing due to fatigue and justified grumblings about the program.

Lunch

Interview lunches range from a meal you buy at the hospital cafeteria to a fancy repast at a downtown restaurant. In any event, eat lightly. If you are stuffed, your concentration and alertness will dissipate as your body focuses on digesting your heavy meal. As with dinner the night before, use lunch as an opportunity to learn more about the program from house staff eating with you and about other programs from your fellow applicants. Avoid messy foods (eg, pasta) that can leave its calling card on your new professional outfit. Because it is tough to maintain a high energy level all day, you might want a cup of coffee or a caffeinated drink to keep you from fading in the afternoon, especially if you have another interview scheduled.

FEAST ON INFORMATION, NOT FOOD.

INTERVIEWING SAVOIR-FAIRE

The interview sessions themselves are usually perceived as the most stressful portion of the interview day. Study after study indicates that these encounters are one of the most important factors in the selection of house staff. Unfortunately, most of these same studies show interviews to have poor predictive value of your future performance as a resident, and show abysmally low reproducibility between interviewers. The bottom line is that the conclusions drawn by an interviewer can often be inaccurate and imprecise. No matter how stellar you are, if the interviewer got up on the wrong side of the bed, you may get toasted anyway. Fortunately for you, interviewers' bad hair days don't happen very often, and most interviews conducted today are low-stress, non-confrontational meetings with a single interviewer. In addition, there are a few things you can do to give yourself the best chance of pulling off a successful interview.

CONCLUSIONS DRAWN BY AN INTERVIEWER CAN BE INACCURATE.

Before the actual interviews, learn the pronunciation of your interviewer's name from the departmental secretary or the interviewer's administrative assistant. Arrive at your interviews a few minutes early. If the waiting room makes you anxious, try different relaxation techniques such as deep, steady breathing or alternately tensing and relaxing different muscle groups. It may help your nervousness to remember that interviews often run behind schedule and that experienced interviewers are aware of this tendency. If you are running late, your subsequent interviewer will understand when you explain that your previous interview just finished. When you meet your interviewer, introduce yourself and offer a firm, confident handshake. After being invited into the office, do not sit down until the interviewer sits or invites you to sit.

DOUBLE-CHECK THE PRONUNCIATION OF YOUR INTERVIEWER'S NAME.

During the interview, maintain fairly constant eye contact with the interviewer. Do not let your gaze or attention wander, especially when the interviewer is speaking directly to you. Do **not** take notes during the interview; write them down later. Try to project a high energy level, even if this is your fifteenth interview. Answer the questions fully yet avoid rambling; if they want to know more about a particular subject, they will ask. If you can, gently steer the interview toward your strong points, but do not pressure the interviewer or dominate the dialogue; leave filibusters to the politicians. Monitor any signs of nervousness, including fidgeting and pressured speech. **Never** peek at your watch, even if you know that the interview is running overtime. When the interview is finished, thank the interviewer, shake hands again and leave gracefully. Make an effort not to fumble with your folder, purse or briefcase as you rise from your chair.

WHAT ARE INTERVIEWERS LOOKING FOR?

No matter what specialty interests you, interviewers often seek the same set of qualities in would-be residents. These include character traits in addition to intellectual abilities.

- ▶ **Intelligence/knowledge.** Does the applicant demonstrate a rich fund of medical knowledge when discussing cases? Is he or she conversant with the history as well as the current issues and challenges defining the specialty?
- ▶ **Enthusiasm/charisma.** Residency directors consider this to be an invaluable commodity, essential to surviving a long, and often demanding residency. Does the applicant demonstrate liveliness and vivacity? Does he or she appear to have stamina and endurance as well?
- ▶ **Maturity/insight:** Does the applicant have realistic and appropriate goals? Are his or her responses measured and well-conceived? Can the applicant appraise himself or herself honestly, addressing both strengths and weaknesses?
- ▶ **Shared philosophy/personality:** Will I enjoy working with this applicant on a regular basis? What do I think this individual will add to this program?

WHAT DO INTERVIEWERS ASK?

We have compiled a list of the most common interview questions, with suggested approaches for responding.

Tell Me About Yourself.

A favorite opener. You can respond by asking whether there is anything specific that they would like to know about you, or whether they would like to hear first about your personal or professional background. Otherwise, a short biographical statement will suffice. Because you are asked to summarize your life on this planet in one breath, program directors expect a sense for what you hold most essential. Highlight any unusual or noteworthy interests or experiences, but again, keep it brief. Two additional pointers may be helpful in answering this question: (1) Stress only positive features; (2) Back up generalities with specific illustrations or examples (eg, if you tell the interviewer that you're "research-oriented," briefly describe 1 or 2 of your projects or publications).

What Are Your Strengths and Weaknesses?

One of the most familiar "tough" questions that surface in interviews. Be ready to summarize your strong points and achievements in three or four concise sentences. The interviewer wants to know whether you can assess your own strengths and weaknesses accurately, and whether you can take appropriate steps to address any deficiencies in your training. The trick is to mention only the deficiencies that tend to be common among your colleagues (eg, weaknesses in ambulatory orthopedics, if you are going into family practice). Do **not** use the worn "my weakness is my strength" ploy. The interviewer will only roll his or her eyes when you "confess" that you are such a perfectionist that you are often unable to leave the hospital before midnight.

Why Are You Interested in Our Program?

Why do you want to come here? Here all your background research and reading pays off. House staff and applicants you meet on the interview circuit can readily identify the strengths and the unique features of the program for you. Stress the philosophies and goals that you have in common with the program, whether dedication to care of the indigent or to high-tech research. If you don't read up on the program before you interview, then you deserve to get burned.

> STRESS PHILOSOPHIES AND GOALS ALSO SHARED BY THE PROGRAM.

What Are You Looking for in a Program?

If you have been actively engaged in your application process, then you should be able to answer this question off the top of your head. The interviewer is primarily assessing whether his or her program can meet **your** needs. Highlight the strengths and unique features that make the program attractive to you; do **not** dwell on the program's lackluster areas.

Why Should We Choose You?

What can you contribute to our program? This is almost the reverse of the previous question. To answer this question, you need to reconcile your understanding of the program with a good sense of your own strengths and goals. For example, if the program has an inner-city setting with a large Hispanic population, mention your long-standing interest in indigent health care and fluency in Spanish.

Can You Tell Me About This Deficiency on Your Record?

The experienced interviewer will be on the lookout for evasions or excuses from applicants who cannot take responsibility for their actions. Be honest and drop the excuses. Be prepared to "take the rap" for any weaknesses in your application. By all means, let the interviewer know if the problem was connected to an unforeseen or unavoidable personal crisis (eg, major illness, divorce, death of a family member). Otherwise, acknowledge the deficiency and offer evidence that you have made a sincere effort to overcome it. If you handle this question well, you will have demonstrated to the interviewer that, while not the perfect applicant (no one is), you have the ability to learn and grow. On the other hand, don't volunteer negative information. Unless you have good reason to believe that something from your past will sink your application, it's poor form to discuss deficiencies not raised by the interviewer.

Why Are You Interested in This Specialty?

What other specialties did you consider and why? The interviewer wants to verify that your reasons for entering this specialty are both reasonable and genuine. You probably know exactly why you chose one specialty over others; however, it is difficult to verbalize your reasoning on a moment's notice. It helps to formulate a brief answer to this question on paper beforehand. A few words of caution: (1) Lifestyle or monetary prospects are generally considered shallow reasons for entering a particular specialty, so be careful about mentioning these considerations; (2) Do not criticize or put down other specialties in the course of explaining your interest in this specialty. You want to convey the impression that you are attracted to the specialty for its positive attributes, not because you were turned off by everything else.

What Do You See Yourself Doing in the Future?

Nobody expects you to know exactly what you want to do after your residency, but interviewers do want evidence that you have considered and planned for the most likely career possibilities. Be ready to explore your motivations for these options.

How Do You Think the Current Changes in Health Care Will Affect the Specialty?

Hopefully, you already asked yourself —and answered—this question when you selected your specialty. If not, you can pick up the current thinking by talking to faculty and house staff in the field or following the specialty journal. Recent changes in health care are unprecedented; and a lot of people are understandably concerned about the long-term implications. Your interviewer will certainly appreciate a well-considered analysis.

Do You Have Any Plans for a Family?

This is an illegal question that constantly crops up in interviews, especially for female applicants. The interview itself is not, however, the time to lecture the interviewer on the finer points of discrimination in hiring. Answer the question honestly if possible. Otherwise, you can handle it by saying simply, "I have no plans for a family at this time."

What Do You Do in Your Spare Time?

The interviewer wants to see if you have a life outside of medicine. This is an opportunity for you to allow your personality to shine through. But—try not to sound more enthusiastic about what you do with your free time than about your commitment to medicine!

Describe an Interesting Case That You Had.

This is a more frequent test of your clinical acumen and your presentation skills. In essence, you are being asked to make a bullet presentation. If this question comes up, begin with a 30-second outline of a case you know well. This should be fully rehearsed but spoken with spontaneity. Lay out the interesting diagnostic or treatment issues facing the team at the time. At this point, the interviewer may join you in a discussion of these issues.

LIFESTYLE AND MONEY ARE GENERALLY CONSIDERED SHALLOW REASONS FOR ENTERING A SPECIALTY.

HOT TOPICS INCLUDE MANAGED CARE, SUPPLY OF SPECIALISTS VERSUS GENERALISTS, AND MEDICARE/MEDICAID REFORM.

WHAT DO I ASK THE INTERVIEWER?

Toward the middle or the end of the session, your interviewer will invariably ask you, "Do you have any questions?" Be prepared in advance with at least two to three questions to show your curiosity and interest, as long as it's appropriate for the interviewer or program. Faculty members can field the more philosophical and broad-based questions like the ones listed below.

An ideal question is one that the interviewer will enjoy answering thus leaving an overall positive tone to the encounter. Remember, however, that you are still the person under observation and evaluation. Do **not** harp on the program's weaknesses. Also, avoid asking questions during the interview about salaries and benefits, vacation, moonlighting, call schedules, and other aspects of the day-to-day operations of the program. Save these practical concerns for the house staff. Keep your interview questions friendly and benign.

Appropriate Questions for Faculty Interviewers

1. What do you like most about your training program? In what areas can the program improve itself?
2. Where have your residents gone after graduation?
3. What process do you have for improving the residency? For evaluating rotations?
4. Have you ever done "post-marketing" surveys of your graduates? What do they tell you?
5. What recent changes has the program undergone? What changes do you foresee?
6. How many clinicians are there in the program? Researchers/academicians?
7. What research opportunities are available? What is the availability of funding for research? What kind of mentor support is available from the faculty?
8. In what direction do you see the chairperson (or residency director) taking the program? Do you believe that he or she will remain here during my residency training?
9. If there is an interim chair: What is the status of the search process? What changes do you foresee in the program as a result of this transition?
10. What other residency programs do you like and recommend? Why?
11. What opportunities are there to attend regional and national conferences and seminars?
12. How well do the residents perform on board certification exams?
13. What is the structure of the last years of residency? Does the program offer elective time? Mini-fellowships? Time and opportunity to work abroad?

WHAT TYPES OF QUESTIONS SHOULD I ASK THE HOUSE STAFF?

We compiled a list of questions that you might ask house staff while you are visiting the program. Most of them deal with the daily operation of the residency. A few, however, are sensitive questions that you might not feel com-

> THE QUESTIONS YOU ASK CAN BE REVEALING TO THE INTERVIEWER.

> NEVER GRILL THE INTERVIEWER.

fortable asking all house staff that you encounter (eg, chief residents steeped in the program's "party line"). The sample questions are organized largely by issues discussed in "What should I be looking for in a program?" (p. 61).

General Questions

1. Are the residents happy? What features of the program do they like or dislike?
2. Would the residents choose the same program again?
3. Does the program have trouble filling all its spots?
4. How strong are the residents? From where did they graduate?

Location

1. Is the program located in a safe part of the city? If not, what's the security system like?
2. What do residents do for fun around here?
3. What advantages are specific to the location (eg, unusual patient population, cultural opportunities, climate, low cost of living, etc.)?

Reputation

1. Do graduates of the program have problems finding jobs?
2. How difficult is it for residents to get a good fellowship?

Education

1. Is the program fully accredited?
2. How are the residents evaluated? By whom?
3. Is there an organized curriculum? What is its emphasis?
4. How many conferences/week are there? Do conferences emphasize practical knowledge or state-of-the-art research?
5. What is the quality of the attendings? What are their responsibilities? Do they get along?
6. How interested are the faculty in the education and welfare of the house staff?
7. What proportion of attendings are private?
8. Are there medical students on the wards? What school(s) do they represent? What are the residents' teaching responsibilities to the students?
9. What research opportunities are there? Are faculty research preceptors readily available?

Work Environment

1. What is the patient load like?
2. What are the typical admissions diagnoses?
3. How many cases are treated by the average resident?
4. Is the caseload sufficiently varied?
5. How much autonomy do residents have to manage patients?
6. What is the patient population like? Ethnicity/language? Socioeconomic status?
7. Is there continuity of care for patients after discharge?
8. What is the extent and quality of the ambulatory experience?
9. How strong is nursing support? Consult services? Radiology?
10. Pathology? Emergency services?

11. How much "scut work" is done by house staff? Are there blood drawing/IV teams?
12. What is the typical call schedule?
13. How does the work environment vary from service to service? From hospital to hospital?
14. How busy are call nights? How much sleep do you usually get?
15. How available are the attendings? Can you call them at night?
16. Is there backup available when you're on call? Is there a nightfloat system?
17. How many hours do you work each week?
18. How much time do you get off each week?

Salary

1. What is the starting salary for an intern? For an R2?
2. What about cost of living in the area?
3. Is moonlighting permitted? If so, how does it work around here?

Benefits

1. What health benefits are available (eg, medical insurance, dental plan, eye plan)?
2. What is the maternity/paternity leave policy?
3. Is life insurance available? Disability insurance?
4. Is parking provided? Is subsidized housing available? What is the vacation schedule setup?

HOW TO KILL AN INTERVIEW

Given all the time, expense, and adrenaline that contribute to your program interviews, you don't want to blow your chances with an ill-considered question or comment. Therefore, we have provided a checklist of problems that can cost you the interview.

1. **Rambling:** Interviewers probably hear enough poorly constructed medical student presentations as it is. If rambling is just another nervous habit for you, then it should evaporate as you gain experience and become more comfortable with the interview process. If this is not the case, make a more conscious effort to provide complete yet focused answers. You may find that practice sessions with a friendly classmate will help you overcome this tendency.

2. **Not listening/not "reading" the interviewer correctly:** It is easy to fade away briefly during an interview, especially after lunch. However, these TIAs can become big problems if you misunderstand a question that you weren't expecting, or if as a result you ask a question about a topic previously discussed by the interviewer. Most "misreads" can be prevented by simply keeping your attention focused. Use verbal and nonverbal clues to tailor your responses (eg, if the interviewer is a businesslike, impersonal type, don't give "touchy-feely" answers).

3. **Inadequate preparation:** Nobody will expect you to know their program through and through, but you should know its basics. Interviewers do not want to waste the time allotted for the interview going over information already available in their printed materials.

TAILOR YOUR RESPONSE TO THE INTERVIEWER.

4. **Grilling the interviewer:** It's true in a philosophical sense that you are interviewing the program as much as they are interviewing you. But be practical: don't put the interviewer on the defensive by harping on the program's weaknesses. If these problem spots are of paramount importance to you, save your concerns for the house staff or raise the issue in a friendly, non-confrontational manner. Interviewers may already be well aware of the weakness, and will be more willing to discuss it if they aren't being made to feel as if they owe you an apology.

5. **Inconsistent/evasive answers:** Answers that don't match up with what you wrote on your application, or that are incomplete will put most interviewers on "red alert." Do emphasize your strengths as well as the clinical and academic interests that you share with the interviewer. Do not exaggerate, lie, or otherwise distort facts. Interviewers expect applicants to be open and honest. Moreover, program directors can and often do verify your claims or credentials by calling colleagues at your school.

6. **Displaying a difficult/quirky personality:** The interviewer is trying to picture you as a junior colleague with whom daily interaction will be necessary. If you come across as domineering, inflexible, temperamental, or eccentric, you will not be making this task a pleasant one.

7. **Pejorative comments about other programs:** Negative statements (especially unsolicited or unsupported digs) about other programs or your own school will be noted as indiscretions that reflect badly on you. The interviewer will wonder what you might say about his or her program at the next place on your tour. The residency community is tight, and the interviewer may very well have colleagues and friends at the programs you just bashed.

8. **Poor interactions with administrative staff/house staff:** It should go without saying that rudeness or lack of consideration for these people will be relayed to the residency selection committee, as a strike against you.

WRAPPING UP THE INTERVIEW DAY

The interview day usually flies by quickly, so it's no surprise if you still have some questions at the end of the day. Not to worry; many residents are happy to give you their pager or home phone numbers and talk with you at greater length after hours.

If you really want to learn more about the program, but cannot stay longer because of other scheduled interviews, speak to the departmental secretary or a house staff member about possible arrangements for a return visit. This will allow you to spend more time on rounds, in clinic or surgery, in conferences and in the surrounding neighborhood. In addition, it will give you an opportunity to confirm or modify your initial impressions of the program.

Be sure to jot down your impressions of the program while they are still fresh in your mind. After you have visited four or five programs, the details will start to blur together. To keep your facts and impressions straight, write down all your thoughts about a program as soon as you can at the end of the day. Use the program evaluation worksheet provided (page 63) if you need something to organize your thoughts. You will thank yourself later when you

DON'T GET LURED INTO BASHING OTHER PROGRAMS.

WRITE DOWN YOUR THOUGHTS ABOUT THE INTERVIEW VISIT RIGHT AWAY.

can rank your programs with organized notes while your classmates are banging their heads against the wall trying to remember which program had the deluxe call rooms with the well-stocked refrigerators and HBO.

FOLLOW-UP LETTERS

Unless your interviewer explicitly tells you not to do so, write a letter to thank the program for its hospitality and to express your continued interest. This typed letter should be composed and mailed no more than a few days after the interview, while memories of the interviews (on your part and theirs) are still fresh. The sincere follow-up letter can help solidify the impression you left on the interviewer before it is washed away by subsequent interviews.

Personalize the letter by mentioning a specific topic that was discussed during the interview. You can also use the letter to update your application file if you recently received any honors or awards. The letter should be addressed to your interviewers. Do not be shy in stating why you liked the program and that you will be ranking it highly—if you plan to do so (See Figure 9–1). If you are a strong applicant who wants to attend a less competitive program because of personal reasons, share them with the interviewer. Keep in mind, however, that the NRMP urges you as a general rule not to tell programs how you are ranking them. Finally, most interviewers will not mind a phone call for follow-up questions, although if you do not have an urgent reason or a specific question for one of your interviewers, follow-up calls to programs can appear pushy.

A THANK-YOU CARD INSTEAD OF A LETTER IS A NICE PERSONAL TOUCH IF YOUR HANDWRITING IS NEAT.

FIGURE 9-1

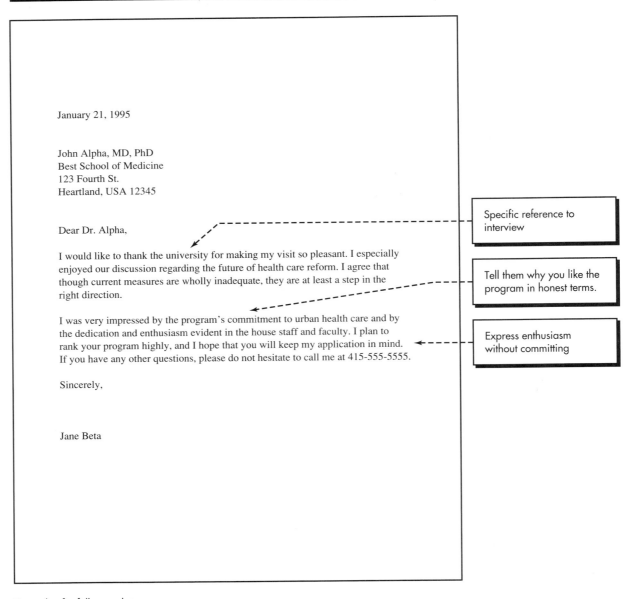

January 21, 1995

John Alpha, MD, PhD
Best School of Medicine
123 Fourth St.
Heartland, USA 12345

Dear Dr. Alpha,

I would like to thank the university for making my visit so pleasant. I especially enjoyed our discussion regarding the future of health care reform. I agree that though current measures are wholly inadequate, they are at least a step in the right direction.

I was very impressed by the program's commitment to urban health care and by the dedication and enthusiasm evident in the house staff and faculty. I plan to rank your program highly, and I hope that you will keep my application in mind. If you have any other questions, please do not hesitate to call me at 415-555-5555.

Sincerely,

Jane Beta

Specific reference to interview

Tell them why you like the program in honest terms.

Express enthusiasm without committing

Example of a follow-up letter.

The Rank List and Match Day

HOW DO I RANK THE PROGRAMS?

Ranking is an important part of the Match process, not to be taken lightly. Year after year, really smart applicants do really stupid things when it comes to ranking programs. Once and for all, there are two rules, and **only** two rules, to keep in mind when you set up your rank list.

Rule #1—Rank programs in order of their desirability. After you have visited all the programs, reviewed your notes, and have weighed all the pros and cons, list the programs in order of their desirability. Enter the programs on your rank list in this exact order. The object is to match with your most desirable program, not to match with your first ranked choice. Do **not** rank a program lower because you believe your chances of attaining that program are slim. Do not rank a program higher because someone said that you were at the top of the program's rank list (see below). Ideally, the programs at the bottom of your rank list will serve as backups—acceptable programs that are a sure bet.

Rule #2—Rank all acceptable programs. After you have completed your interviews, you should have only two categories of programs: acceptable and unacceptable. **Do not rank any programs that you wouldn't want to work in.** Remember that you are under contract to report to the program where you match. If the program is on your rank list at all, you're telling the NRMP that you are willing to go to that program if you match there. You are under no obligation to rank every program that you visit. You must decide, however, whether it is better to match at a less than ideal program or to take your chances in the Scramble if you do not match. The latter option, though highly undesirable, is certainly viable in specialties which have a large number of unfilled positions on Match Day, such as anesthesiology.

The two rules we have given you do not guarantee a match, they guarantee only that you will do the best you can do with what you have to work with (Table 10–1). If you are having a tough time putting all your information together, walk through your rank list with your significant other, friend, or career adviser.

The NRMP Matching Algorithm

The same algorithm is used by the Canadian Residency Matching Service (CaRMS). Outlined below is a simplified explanation of the NRMP algorithm. Your *NRMP Handbook* describes the steps in greater detail.

1. In the first round, programs extend a number of offers to the candidates at the top of their lists. The number of offers extended by the program is equal to the number of slots it has available. For example, a program with 15 first-year slots can extend only 15 offers to the top 15 candidates on its rank list.

2. If the program is on a targeted applicant's rank list, there is then a tentative match. If the applicant receives multiple offers in this round, the tentative match is made with the program highest on his/her rank list, and offers from lower-ranked programs are rejected.

3. In the next round, programs that did not tentatively fill all their slots (ie, some or all of their offers were rejected) extend offers equal to the number of unfilled slots to the next group of applicants on their rank list. For example, if a program failed to fill 4 of its 15 slots in the previous round, it can make up to 4 offers to the next 4 applicants on its rank list.

4. If the program is on the applicant's rank list and he/she has no current offer, then there is a tentative match. If the applicant has an offer from the previous round, there are 2 possible outcomes: (1) either the offer is rejected if the program is ranked lower, or (2) the offer is tentatively accepted if the program is ranked higher, in which case the earlier offer is rejected. That slot is then offered in the next round.

5. The algorithm repeats until all positions are filled or the program runs out of candidates to whom positions can be offered. At this point, the acceptances are considered final.

In short, the program offers positions "down" its rank list of applicants, while applicants accept positions "up" their rank lists, until the applicant is matched to the most desirable program that offered him/her a position. In other words, a tentative match establishes a "floor" for the applicant. He/she can only move higher up the rank list as the algorithm repeats. Note that no applicant can be bypassed by a lower-ranked applicant for a certain program. If the higher-ranked applicant did not tentatively match there, it's because the applicant already had a more desirable offer in hand. Since the algorithm was computerized in 1974, the process takes only minutes to run.

Is the NRMP Algorithm Fair?

The NRMP matching algorithm has worked well since the 1950s and has survived largely intact. However, there have been some recent questions raised about its fairness. This debate was featured in 4 articles in the June

1995 issue of *Academic Medicine*. After reviewing the articles, we've drawn these conclusions:

1. The matching algorithm is not completely neutral. There are a few situations that can result in 2 stable matches, one more favorable to the student and the other more favorable to the hospital. In these situations, the algorithm defaults to the match more favorable to the hospital. According to Kevin Williams, MD, the man who brought the controversy to the forefront, this "tie-breaker" situation occurs with approximately 0.1% of all applicants. If the algorithm defaulted in the applicant's favor, some applicants would match higher on their rank lists. Though the NRMP matching algorithm will be reassessed, there are no current plans to modify the algorithm. Specialty matches outside the NRMP Match are also reevaluating their algorithm. In fact, starting in 1997, the ophthalmology match will switch to an applicant favorable algorithm.

2. In **a few** situations, you can improve your final rank in the Match by **not** ranking all acceptable programs. However, by not ranking all acceptable programs, you increase your chances of not matching at all. Thus, until better information comes along, you should adhere to the two cardinal rules of ranking discussed above.

Bottom line. Is the NRMP Match algorithm unfair? "Unfair" is subjective in this case. It is more accurate to say that the algorithm favors hospitals in "tie-breaker" situations. Will it affect you? At one in a thousand odds, it is extremely unlikely. Should you worry about it? Probably not. You are much more likely to get hurt by a poorly thought out rank list than the current match algorithm.

How do couples rank programs?

The *NRMP Handbook* includes a step-by-step guide for creating a couples rank list. The advice is generally sound. You and your partner should first rank programs as if you were matching on your own. Turn to "How do I rank the programs?" above for guidelines. Then, you should list the possible program pairs if you are ranking more than one program in the same city. In addition to program pairs in the same city/area (Type 1), there are 2 other types of program pairs to consider: pairs of programs not in the same city/area (Type 2) and combinations in which one partner goes unmatched (Type 3). Consider creating and ranking Type 2 pairings if separation is tolerable. These pairs allow both partners to match semi-independently. Because Type 2 pairings are not restricted by geography, the number of possible permutations is large. Consider creating and ranking Type 3 pairings if it is acceptable for one to match and the other to enter the Scramble. This is usually preferable to both of you going unmatched.

Ranking the program pairs is a classic process of give-and-take. Fortunately, the process can be less painful if you and your partner have communicated well during the application process, and thus have a understanding of each other's preferences. Couples must decide how much weight to give the location versus the programs. Regardless, the process may take a few evenings. After all, your rank list can easily be over a hundred pairs long. When ranking Type 3 pairings, factor in the location; it will be easier for the unmatched partner to scramble in a large city with many training programs.

THE ALGORITHM CONTROVERSY IS A TEMPEST IN A TEAPOT.

RANKING A COUPLES LIST IS AN EXERCISE IN OPEN COMMUNICATIONS AND COMPROMISE.

You can register for the couples match when both of you enter your couples list.

Supplemental Rank Order Lists

When an applicant ranks an advanced position (which begins 15 months after the Match), he or she also submits a ranking of PGY-1 (transitional or preliminary) programs on a Supplemental Rank Order List (SROL). The applicant can submit more than one SROL, thus tailoring PGY-1 preferences depending on the location of the advanced training. If you do not match into an advanced position, then your SROLs will not be used. If you go unmatched on your SROL, your advanced match result still holds. You can rank up to 15 programs on your SROLs combined at no charge.

"We are ranking you at the top of our list" (Not!)

Programs often send candidates follow-up letters after the interview to affirm their interest. Sometimes they will assure you that you will be ranked at the top of their list. This may be a pleasant compliment; however, do **not** count on it, and do **not** let it affect your ranking of their program. Even if they say this, it simply means that you can match no lower than that program. Some applicants have an instinctive but unfortunate tendency to favor programs that they believe are more likely to take them. Other applicants allow these follow-up letters to limit the length of their rank list inappropriately. Again, all acceptable programs should be on your rank list.

Under-the-Table Deals

In some of the most competitive fields, program directors or department chairs often call applicants after the interview but before Match Day to ask the applicant about his or her ranking of the program. **It is a violation of Match rules for programs to ask you for this information.** Your ranking of programs should have absolutely no effect on a program's ranking of you. Unless the caller represents your top choice, the question is only a golden opportunity for you to hang yourself. If you tell the program you are not ranking them first, they might drop you on their rank list to ensure that they get their top picks. Believe it or not, some programs would rather minimize how low they go on their rank list instead of just going for their top candidates. If you receive such a call from one of your top choices, **get a commitment in writing from the residency director.** If they balk, then all bets are off. Otherwise, consider telling them that you expect to rank them #1 or very highly even if you are not. After the Match, consider reporting this violation to your Dean of Students, the NRMP or the appropriate specialty board.

Entering Your Rank Order List

Turning in your rank list can feel like asking someone to marry you. You're absolutely sure until the moment you turn in that piece of paper. Then you start thinking, "Wait a minute. Did I do the right thing?" But it's too late; you have already sent the list. Most of the soul-searching and turmoil focuses on the order of your top three choices. Hold on to your list until you can think this through. Discuss strengths and weaknesses of these three programs with your significant other or a close friend. Is it too late to modify the rank list after you have turned it in? Well, actually, no. The NRMP will accept faxed changes for a few days after the deadline has passed, if your Dean of

Students makes a request on your behalf. But—because exercising this option is disruptive and depends heavily on your dean, don't view it as an opportunity to allow you to mull over your rank list past the deadline. **Use this option as a last resort only.**

MARCH MATCHNESS ("IT'S AWESOME, BABY!")

The NRMP Match itself is run in late February. The results are known to your dean's office several days before Match Day, which is usually on a Wednesday in mid-March. The Monday or Tuesday before Match Day is the moment of truth for most. If you do **not** hear from your dean's office during this period, you can assume that you matched. If you fear the worst, you can call your dean's office or the NRMP 2 days before Match Day to learn if you matched. If you did, then you must wait until Match Day itself to find out where you matched. If you do learn that you did not match, please read on for information about the Scramble.

A list of matched independent applicants by code is published in *USA Today* on Unmatch Day (the day before Match Day). If you are an independent candidate and your code is **not** listed, call the NRMP after 9 AM (EST) to confirm your match status.

At medical schools on Match Day, the results are announced simultaneously across the nation at noon, Eastern Standard Time. Many schools organize ceremonies or more casual breakfasts around this event; applicants often bring their significant others to provide moral support and to share in the anticipation. The atmosphere is usually electric by the time the signal is given to open the envelope.

WHAT HAPPENS IF I DON'T MATCH? THE SCRAMBLE

If the news is bad, the fact that you did not match does not amount to a personal rejection from the entire medical profession. It might help your bruised ego to recognize that failure to match is most often due to a poorly thought-out rank list or simply applying in a small competitive specialty. It might also be comforting to know that you are not alone: about a thousand U.S. medical students and several thousand non-U.S. medical student applicants enter the Scramble every year; most of them find quality residency positions immediately.

For better or worse, you'll have to postpone your moping and self-pity till later. You will be apprised of your situation by your dean on Unmatch Day or the day before. You will also be given an *NRMP Results* book that lists programs in your specialty with unfilled positions. You may be able to meet with your adviser or your department chairperson, who can review the NRMP results and quickly draw up a "hot" list of programs for you to pursue. In many cases, your adviser or department chair will intervene and contact program directors on your behalf. **Note that you are not restricted by specialty.** Many applicants decide to pursue additional programs in another specialty because there are too few Scramble positions available in their initial specialty selection (eg, surgery).

If your adviser is unavailable, or if you are not a U.S. medical student, then you will have to contact the programs directly. After you make your list

PRANK CALLS FROM CLASSMATES PRETENDING TO BE FROM THE DEAN'S OFFICE ARE NOT FUNNY.

NOW IS NOT THE TIME TO PANIC!

of programs in order of interest, then track down the program phone numbers in AMA-FREIDA or the Green Book. You can also look up the area code of that program and call information, (area code) 555-1212, to get the local number. You will then need to assemble the following documents for a faxable application file:

- ► Dean's letter
- ► Transcript
- ► A copy of the NRMP Universal Application
- ► Your CV
- ► Any letters of recommendation that you may have

Begin your quest by calling programs in the order in which they appear on your "hot list," starting at noon EST on Unmatch Day. The day will be hectic and stressful; steel yourself for busy signals and harried program secretaries. You will have to make a conscious effort to remain calm and friendly. You will need to fax your application file to interested programs. Your dean's office or the department in your specialty should give you full access to their phones and fax machines. Positions will be offered by phone. If you are offered a position at a program which is low on your "hot list," ask them how long they are willing to hold that position for you. Otherwise, be prepared to wrap up your acceptance over the phone. Most unmatched seniors are placed within a day.

After the Match

THE DAY AFTER

The aftermath of Match Day is not unlike the day after an election. Even if you're ecstatic about the outcome, you can't just party for a week; there are tasks to be performed, such as gearing up for your new position and thanking your supporters. You want your new associates to be glad they "elected" you. So shake off the hangover and. . . .

Call your program, first of all, to introduce yourself in an enthusiastic manner as one of the incoming interns. Ask for the "class" roster; chances are you'll know a few of them either from your school or from the interview trail. Then find out who the chief residents will be. Inquire about scheduling. Are there any electives? Will you have any say in balancing easy and tough months? How are vacation days assigned? This is also the time to mention any non-negotiable schedule constraints, such as your upcoming wedding. In addition, ask what information or credentials they would like from you. Some of the more academic programs have some prerequisite reading before the program begins. It's also important to ask about their ACLS/ATLS training policy. Some programs expect you to come with certification in hand; others will put you through an ACLS course when you start.

After your introductory contact, write thank-you letters to the program director and to your interviewers. They were your advocates during the rough-and-tumble ranking sessions. When they receive letters from you, they will be assured that they made the right choice. Plus: don't forget to thank your advisers and all those at your school who supported you with letters of recommendation. They would like to know where their support landed you. Take the time to give them honest feedback so that they can adjust their advice for future students.

> IN MOST INTERNSHIPS, YOUR SCHEDULE IS YOUR LIFE.

WHAT IF I'M NOT HAPPY WITH MY MATCH RESULT?

The good news is that over 80% of U.S. seniors will get one of their first three choices in the Match. Even if you did not match at one of your top choices, however, you should have few regrets if you followed the two cardi-

TABLE 11-1. Essential residency contract terms.
• Resident's responsibilities
• Salary and other stipends
• Other benefits
• Length of contract and terms of renewal
• Policies for sick leave, parental leave, etc.
• Grievance and sexual harassment policies

"IF YOU CAN'T BE WITH THE ONE YOU LOVE, LOVE THE ONE YOU'RE WITH."

nal matching rules outlined in Chapter 10. First of all, be reassured that feelings of insecurity are a normal reaction to major life decisions. This case of the jitters is commonly known as "buyer's remorse." Our advice is to relax; the feelings should pass. Secondly, remember that your participation in the NRMP Match means at least a 1-year commitment to the program.

THE RESIDENCY CONTRACT

After the Match, you will receive a residency contract to sign and return to your program. The Accreditation Council for Graduate Medical Education (ACGME) recommends that certain terms and conditions be clearly addressed in the contract (Table 11–1). Before you sign your contract, **understand the definitions of all essential terms.**

GETTING SET UP

Moving right along . . . your next set of priorities is relocating. Nobody enjoys the process, but it doesn't have to be the mother of all battles either. Some choice pointers:

Housing Tips

Housing should be arranged before graduation if at all possible. First: Explore the pros and cons of renting versus buying; housing costs vary widely across the United States, and a good deal for one area may not be your best bet in another. Often it's best to talk to the current house staff at your program about their impressions of the local market. As long as you can afford the payments, buying a small home or a condo may make investment sense if you plan to stay in the area for several years. On the other hand, renting will give you the flexibility to look for bigger and better places after you have a chance to size up the area. For the first year, it's safest to focus on finding a short-commute, hassle-free situation, as every hour is precious during internship.

There are many ways to find housing opportunities: (1) Call up friends who live near the program for housing tips; (2) Ask the residency office about housing options; (3) Visit a realty service or a professional rental service; (4) Go to the local library and search the classifieds in a newspaper from your new city. Listings available through rental and roommate agencies tend to be of higher quality since the listing fee is self-selecting. Unless it's a huge hassle, plan to visit the city for at least 2 to 4 days, to find and finalize housing arrangements.

TABLE 11-2. Packing essentials check list.

- ☐ Packing boxes
- ☐ Newspapers
- ☐ Plastic/bubble wrap
- ☐ Cord/rope
- ☐ Packing tape
- ☐ Scissors
- ☐ Utility knife
- ☐ Markers
- ☐ Labels

Moving Tips

In anticipation for your move, prepare change of address cards and arrange mail forwarding with the Post Office. For tracking purposes, you should make a catalog of your belongings (if you have a lot of material you might organize it by room) and photograph valuable items for insurance purposes. Selling or donating all non-essential belongings will streamline the move and your life in the long run. In addition, make sure you have adequate packing materials before you start the job (Table 11–2). If you are on a tight budget, boxes can usually be harvested in waste disposal areas behind the hospital. Boxes for IV bottles have dividers and are perfect for glassware. Alternatively, many grocery stores or liquor stores will donate their large cardboard boxes, sturdy enough for packing books. Furniture stores are typically more than happy to supply you with large sheets of leftover plastic and bubble wrap.

You have several options for moving your stuff once it's packed. If you have little or no furniture (or none worth taking), then your moving will be easy. Just pack your nonbreakable belongings and call UPS at (800) PICK-UPS for a pickup. UPS does have a limit on the maximum size and weight per box, so call for details. The company automatically insures goods for up to $100 per box and sells insurance for belongings of greater value. Move your valuable or more fragile items personally.

If you have furniture worth keeping, then you might want to move it yourself. There are a number of self-moving companies with one-way moving vans, like Ryder and U-Haul. If you contact a local branch of such a company rather than the central office, you can often bargain for the truck/van rental. This is the cheaper way to move; however, beware of the hassle factor. It's worth considering hiring professional movers to do the job; it costs more, but you'll avoid piling the stress of moving your belongings on top of starting your internship.

Settling Down

By all means, take a vacation; but give yourself at least 1 or 2 weeks to settle into your new home before the start of internship. You will need this block of time to set up your household, open bank accounts, turn on utilities, and install a telephone line. If you wait to show up 2 days before a very busy internship begins, it may take you the next 2 months just to unpack. Extra time will also give you a chance to explore the neighborhood and city before internship takes over your life. You won't want to waste time later locating grocery stores, affordable restaurants, 24-hour gas stations, and the like. Try to streamline all non-medical aspects of life (eg, bill paying, shopping) so that your time off is "quality time."

THERE IS NO BETTER TIME TO SIMPLIFY YOUR LIFE.

LICENSING

The Match is over; you've moved into a nice apartment five minutes from the hospital. Now all you have to do is brace for internship, right? Wrong. During the throes of internship, you will have to apply for **licensure,** the **USMLE Step 3,** and **DEA registration.** Unfortunately, these applications require you to fill out a mountain of paperwork and involve such things as notarized documents, fingerprints and birth certificates. Thus, the preparation you begin **before** starting internship will minimize your stress and vastly enhance your ability to become licensed when you want to be or are required to be.

The tips on the following pages were provided by Licensure Unlimited to help you get started. Licensure Unlimited is a professional service that specializes in managing application processes for physicians. Armed with this information, you will be able to control all three of these critical processes so that you can become licensed in a timely fashion with a minimum number of surprises (e.g., deadlines, exam dates, and required fees). Alternatively, if you desire additional assistance, you can contact Licensure Unlimited at:

Licensure Unlimited
4023 Lincoln Ave
Culver City, CA 90232
(800) 838-1979

What Is Licensure?

"Licensure" is the legal term that denotes approval to practice medicine. It is granted by a governing body on the basis of the laws in your jurisdiction. Some states offer several types of licensure—e.g., training, military, inactive, locum tenens, temporary, or permanent. Periods of licensure also vary from state to state; some licenses are valid for only one year, others for two. Similarly, some licenses can be renewed after a set period of time that is based on your birthdate, while others are renewable on an annual basis during a particular month of the year.

You should also be aware that in some states, the medical board can fine residents and programs up to $2500 for failing to obtain licensure as defined by the law. In support of this legislation, some programs have even been known to terminate house staff who fail to become licensed by state-mandated deadlines.

DO NOT MAKE YOUR NEED TO BE LICENSED AN EMERGENCY FOR THE MEDICAL BOARD.

You should also remember that medical boards process thousands of applications each year, usually on a first-come, first-served basis. They will **not** process files that are out of order **for any reason whatsoever.** So be courteous when discussing your application with licensing technicians, and allow for plenty of time.

Most residents will also want to avoid using their vacations for completing applications—although the latest information indicates that fully one-third of all residents nonetheless wait until the midpoint of their internships to begin reviewing issues surrounding licensure.

Once you have matched, we recommend that you obtain the regulations for licensure in the state where you will be training. Then carefully review those regulations, paying particular attention to USMLE Step 3 exam dates and deadlines, when you are eligible for licensure, and when you are required to be licensed in your jurisdiction.

Steps Toward Licensure

The following tips will help further your goal of obtaining licensure in a straightforward and timely manner. Contact the state board before internship to obtain licensure information. Once you know the deadlines, start the licensure application process **six months** before the licensure deadline in your state. Before you Perma-Plaque or frame your medical school diploma, be sure to make 10 copies of it on 8 1/2- by 11-inch paper. Send all forms via certified, registered or express mail, or enclose prepaid postcards to allow for acknowledgment of materials received. When dealing with medical board personnel, be very courteous (they're just like residency application secretaries: cross them and you're history) and honest about your background.

The Nitty Gritty

Once you know what is required for licensure in your jurisdiction, you can prepare for the application process by doing some or all of the following, as appropriate:

- ► Identify the location and cost of **photographic services.** Be sure to find a photographic service near your place of work, as you may need to make a couple of visits there during work hours.
- ► Identify the location and cost of a **notary public.** If there is no notary public in your facility, try real-estate offices or banks. Be aware, however, that many notary publics have limited hours of availability. Also be sure to complete your application before obtaining notarization, but **do not sign the application** until you are in the presence of the notary. A valid picture ID will also be required—e.g., a driver's license or a passport.
- ► Identify the location and cost of fingerprinting services.
- ► Identify potential personal references, and then contact them to discuss their willingness to serve as references on your behalf.
- ► Research the addresses and costs of obtaining academic transcripts.
- ► List all hospitals and addresses where staff privileges have been granted.
- ► Order a certified copy of your birth certificate.
- ► If you have changed your name, locate and obtain documentation which will verify that change.

Obstacles to Licensure

Potential obstacles to licensure that **both U.S. and international medical graduates** may face are as follows:

- • **Missing critical deadlines**—e.g., failure to apply for and take the USMLE Step 3 in conjunction with licensing deadlines. Since one of the primary requirements for licensure is successful completion of the USMLE Step 3, you must time the Step 3 exam so that you take it at least three months prior to your licensure deadline. This will allow for the scoring of your exam as well as for the reporting of your scores to the medical board. Another benefit of taking the exam early is that it allows you time to take it again should that prove necessary.

- **Failure to include correct licensure/exam fees along with your application.** Most medical boards will return your application if the fees you enclosed are incorrect. You should also be aware that most application fees are nonrefundable.

- **Failure to provide complete and accurate information on your application.** In reviewing your application, medical boards sometimes uncover discrepancies such as inconsistently reported attendance dates. If this is the case, the board must write you a letter explaining the discrepancy they found and what you must do to rectify it.

- **Incomplete documentation.** As is the case with all bureaucracies, forms are not always completed properly by other institutions. Unfortunately, however, incomplete forms sent to the medical board by your undergraduate school, medical school, or training program will be returned to you to correct. You may then need to call the facility where the error occurred to ensure that the forms are properly handled the second time around.

- **Submitting unrequested documentation to the medical board.** Documents that have not been requested but are enclosed with your application can confuse and frustrate licensing technicians. Moreover, the inclusion of such documents in your application package can raise troubling questions both about your application and about your ability to follow basic instructions.

- **Administrative holds on transcripts.** Transcripts can be held for a variety of reasons, including delinquent student loans, unpaid library fines, and the like.

- **Administrative holds by training programs.** Program directors may deny your request to complete your licensure form on the basis of incomplete patient chart dictations, etc. (This is rare, but it has been known to occur.)

- **Disregarding requests for additional documentation.** Requests for additional documentation by the medical board are commonplace but should not be ignored, as some states consider a file closed if it has not been fully completed within a certain period of time. Thus, you should provide all documentation requested in a timely manner.

- **Failing to report a change of address to the medical board.** Most states will not forward licenses in the mail. Thus, if you have recently moved, be sure to notify your medical board of your new address **in writing** at the earliest possible time.

- **Failing to keep copies of documents that are submitted to the medical board.** It is always a good idea to keep extra copies of all forms and their addresses. That will help you track lost documents while also helping resolve questions the board might have on a particular document.

- **Exhibiting abusive behavior toward medical board personnel.** Medical board personnel typically have a very large workload. Thus, working cooperatively with them is clearly in your best interests. Remember, board personnel don't make the licensing laws; they're just chartered to uphold them.

- **Starting the application process too late.** If you are not licensed by the deadline set by your state medical board, you may be unable to continue your training program.

The following potential obstacles to licensure apply to **international medical graduates** (IMGs) only:

- **Getting forms completed by a foreign medical school.** Documents sent to foreign medical schools often require additional processing time. It can thus be highly advantageous to have someone living near your medical school oversee the process of document completion, mailing, etc.
- **Failure to complete sufficient hours in required clinical rotations.** IMGs should carefully review licensing requirements for the state from which they are requesting licensure.
- **Inadequate documentation of individual clinical rotations.** Some states have their own individual forms to be used for documenting each rotation. Again, contact your medical board for details.
- **Failure to use medical-board-approved translators for documents written in other languages.** Some state medical boards have a list of translators whom they have deemed acceptable for translating application documents. Contact your medical board for more information.

First Aid for the USMLE Step 3

The USMLE is the primary licensing examination for physicians and, as such, has replaced both the NBME and the FLEX. The USMLE Step 3 is offered twice a year—once in May and once in December (Table 11-3). Your eligibility to take the USMLE Step 3 is based on your having passed the USMLE Step 1 and 2 or an equivalent combination of prior NBME and FLEX exams. Check with your state medical board for further details.

Be sure to plan ahead for the USMLE Step 3. Although the cost of taking the exam is a fixed $300, some states add administrative charges to this overall cost. These extra charges can, moreover, vary from state to state, since some state medical boards conduct the Step 3 examination themselves while others rely on the USMLE to do so. The application for Step 3 also differs somewhat from those for the USMLE Step 1 and 2—e.g., your signature must be notarized, and additional documents may be required. International medical graduates must, in addition, be certified by the ECFMG or have successfully completed a Fifth Pathway program. You can use Express Mail, Federal Express, or UPS to deliver your application, but faxed documents are unacceptable. Be sure to make copies of all documents, and keep in mind that it takes six to eight weeks to score the exam. The following are some basic administrative guidelines to follow in preparing to take the USMLE Step 3:

- **Call your state medical board for a USMLE Step 3 application, and read it carefully.** Experience has taught that it is critical to verify when you are eligible to take the Step 3 exam, as this may vary from state to

TABLE 11–3. USMLE Step 3 Test Dates.
May 13–14, 1997
December 2–3, 1997
May 12–13, 1998
December 1–2, 1998

state. One state, for example, previously required Step 3 examinees to have completed nine months of postgraduate training before taking the exam. This meant that interns in that state were ineligible to take the Step 3 exam in December of their internship year. Even if you do find you are eligible to take the December Step 3 exam, you should be aware that deadlines for applications start as early as August or September of your internship year.

- **Start the application process early.** Application deadlines of 90 to 120 days prior to the exam date are typical, so start the application process for the USMLE Step 3 a minimum of two months prior to the USMLE application deadline in your state (see Table 11–3). It has been our experience that exceptions are not made for application deadlines.
- **Find out when your state requires you to be licensed and whether that date differs from that of your training program's requirement.** To help you determine when to take Step 3, work backward from your state licensure deadline to determine which exam date you should schedule. Be sure to factor in the six to eight weeks that it will take for scoring and notification of results.
- **Locate a photographic service for required application photos.**
- **Identify a notary public in your facility to obtain required notarizations.**
- **Oh, yeah, don't forget to study.**

DON'T FORGET TO WRITE

Congratulations! You've made it to internship. We hope that the advice and information in this book was helpful. Much of what you have read comes from the experiences of students who have gone before you. We hope that you'll share the lessons you have learned with those to follow, by e-mailing us or sending in the contribution forms (pp xv–xx). As for internship, nothing can save you from that. But don't worry—in a year, you'll be done (or done in). Best of luck.

Index